PRAISE FOR
YOU WILL MAKE MISTAKES

"Leneé really hits the mark in her debut title, *You Will Make Mistakes*. As Christians, we tend to demand perfection of ourselves, as if any missteps are evidence of a lack of faith and obedience. This can create constant crushing pressure to perform. With scriptural support, practical advice, and vivid storytelling, Leneé makes a compelling case to give us permission to be human and walk in God's grace throughout life's inevitable challenges."

—Kati Kleber, Author, Nurse Educator,
and Owner of FreshRN.com

"Not only does this book reveal the heart behind perfectionism, but it also provides keys to free yourself from its chains. You'll find yourself resonating with the author's personal experiences one minute and the next, overwhelmed with *aha!* moments as Pezzano links scriptural references with what the Holy Spirit taught her. A must-read for any Christian!"

—Renee Vidor, Author of *Measuring Up:
How to Win in a World of Comparison*

"Thank you, Leneé, for your transparency and willingness to be vulnerable in an effort to connect with your audience and guide them toward freedom and personal empowerment. This book truly captures the essence of God's grace."

—Cheryl Rice, PhD, educator, and inspired friend

"Leneé takes a vulnerable and compassionate approach to a topic that can be very difficult for so many. Individuals at all levels of their faith can benefit from her incredible insight into the heart of God and practical steps toward discovering God's grace through their own relationship with Him."

—Chris Borja, Founder of Become a Better Networker, the Connected Networking Group, and Borja Virtual, LLC

"Leneé Pezzano's book, *You Will Make Mistakes: Discovering God's Grace in the Midst of Perfectionism,* is a must-read for those struggling with perfectionism versus God's grace. In section three, *The Recipe for Freedom,* Leneé states, 'True freedom is found when we partner with God in the process.' Leneé shares her life's journey in understanding when one partners with God, grace becomes a process of discovery."

—Sandy Burkett, PhD, Co-founder of Breakthrough Reconciliation Ministries and Breakthrough Biblical Counseling

"If you are ready to break the bondage of perfectionism in your life, then I implore you to read this book. I promise you'll experience new levels of God's grace you may not have seen before, and in the process, you'll start seeing the chains of perfectionism come flying off! I know it did for me, and I pray the same for you."

—Jeff Elder, Founder of Business God's Way

YOU WILL MAKE MISTAKES

YOU WILL MAKE MISTAKES

Discovering God's Grace in the Midst of Perfectionism

Leneé Pezzano

AUTHOR ACADEMY elite

Published by Author Academy Elite
PO Box 43, Powell, OH 43065
AuthorAcademyElite.com

Identifiers:
Library of Congress Control Number: 2022917383
Softcover ISBN: 979-8-88583-138-3
Hardcover ISBN: 979-8-88583-139-0
E-book ISBN: 979-8-88583-140-6

Available in paperback, hardback, and e-book.

All Scripture quotations, unless otherwise indicated, are taken from the following versions:

Scripture quotations marked (ASV) are taken from the American Standard Version Bible (Public Domain).
Scripture marked AMPC are taken from the Amplified Bible Copyright © 1954, 1958, 1962, 1964, 1965, 1987 by The Lockman Foundation, La Habra, CA 90631. All rights reserved.
Complete Jewish Bible Copyright © 1998 by David H. Stern. All rights reserved. No portion of this book may be reproduced, stored in a retrieval system, or transmitted in any form or by any means without prior written permission of the publisher.
English Standard Version®, ESV®. Copyright © 2001 by Crossway, a publishing ministry of Good News Publishers. Used by permission.
Scripture quotations marked (KJV) are taken from the KING JAMES VERSION, public domain.
The Holy Bible, New American Standard Version®, NASB®. Copyright © 1995, 2020 by The Lockman Foundation.™ Used by permission. All rights reserved worldwide.
The Holy Bible, New International Version®, NIV®. Copyright © 1973, 1978, 1984 by Biblica, Inc.™ Used by permission. All rights reserved worldwide.
Scripture taken from the New King James Version®, NKJV®. Copyright © 1982 by Thomas Nelson. Used by permission. All rights reserved.

Any Internet addresses (websites, blogs, etc.) printed in this book are offered as a resource. They are not intended in any way to be or imply an endorsement by Author Academy Elite, nor does Author Academy Elite vouch for the content of these sites and numbers for the life of this book.

Some names and identifying details have been changed to protect the privacy of individuals.

DEDICATION

This book is dedicated to my sweet mom, Carol Jean.
You are dearly loved and missed.

CONTENTS

PART 1
THE RULES

PART 2
THE REMEDY

PART 3
THE RECIPE FOR FREEDOM

PART 4
THE RENEWAL

FOREWORD

In March 2020, I found myself preparing to attend an online church meeting hosted by friends of mine in Illinois. It was in the midst of the government shutdown due to the Covid virus, and like all of you, I was looking for ways to stay close to friends and family and connect in meaningful ways. While most of the attendees were from Illinois, some people joined from Ohio, North Carolina, and myself, at the time, from Texas. While I had known my friends for years, everyone else I was meeting for the first time. After a discussion of Scripture and prayer, we began to talk more intimately as a group and discuss life as it was.

Leneé was one of my new acquaintances. She is a beautiful woman with long, flowing brown curls that frame a glowing sun-kissed face adorned with large, compelling eyes and a smile that will brighten anyone's day. She possesses the raw, natural beauty that Solomon so passionately describes as the physical attributes of his lover in Song of Solomon. When she first spoke, I knew I was going to like her. It was clear to me that she was a professional who handled herself well, spoke with consideration and kindness, was mature in her reasoning, and, while sharp-witted, had a genuineness that made her approachable. It was an immediate connection as an entrepreneur and professional for over 40 years. But what truly brought us together was our love of God and the desire to spread the Good News of that love to others!

We spent hours getting to know each other, sharing stories, discussing life, advising each other on business matters, laughing, crying, and praying together on a regular basis. My daughter and I even flew to Illinois to visit our mutual friends, and Leneé drove over from Ohio so we could finally meet face to face. It was a time filled with good fellowship, laughter, and great Italian cooking! Leneé impresses in the kitchen as only an Italian can, and my daughter now regularly makes Leneé's homemade manicotti recipe!

In my own life, God had begun to unfold a vision to me concerning the development of a retreat where people would come to find comfort, whether that be in the form of food, shelter, or companionship. While the retreat is multifaceted, one of the more profound aspects is an offering to those in hospice care. Those without family or a nice place to spend their last days are invited to come and stay at the retreat free of charge, surrounded by beauty and those who care so that they may be loved on and pass with dignity. As the vision began to unfold, the steps were taken to create a 501(c)(3) nonprofit, and The Delsa was birthed. Needing a board of directors, it was vital to the success of the vision that the board members be comprised of true disciples of Yeshua and that they would be prayer warriors for the work that lay ahead. Leneé was one of five that lay on my heart, and I was blessed and encouraged when she accepted.

As our friendship and business ventures continued to entwine our lives, what began to unfold was that we shared similar struggles in our walk with God. Leneé was a true friend and confidante, and I found great comfort in discussing the various challenges, talking through Scripture that always pointed us to the truth, and praying for each other that, ". . . *the One who began a good work among you will keep it growing until it is completed on the Day of the Messiah Yeshua*" (Philippians 1:6, CJB).

In Leneé's own life, God had given her a vision as well. She had known for a few years that she would be writing a book, and as God unfolded the message to her, she was faithful to pick up the pen and write. As she worked on the final draft, she reached out to a group of people, asking that they read through the draft and give feedback. I was honored to be a part of that team and relished being one of the first to savor the words that flowed from this woman's love of God and experience the compassion, understanding, and mercy He was pouring out to his people through this message. I found as I turned each page that my heart was stirred with conviction, and as the tears fell silently, I found words of hope, words of power, and words of joy for my own life. Leneé's personal insight into the struggles of a perfectionist, how God views this cruel taskmaster, and His ultimate deliverance from this bondage into the Kingdom of God has been woven into a beautiful cloak that I hope you will be able to slip your arms into as I did, and wrap it around you as a gentle reminder that you are loved and cherished, a child of God, and that you can trust Him—always.

*"Many people who heard him say these things trusted in him. So, Yeshua said to the Judeans who had trusted him. 'If you obey what I say, then you are really my disciples, **you will know the truth, and the truth will set you free.**'"* (John 8:30–32, CJB, emphasis added)

*". . . be satisfied with what you have; **for God himself has said, 'I will never fail you or abandon you.'** Therefore, we say with confidence, 'Yehovah is my helper; I will not be afraid—what can a human being do to me?' Remember . . . those who spoke God's message to you. **Reflect on the results of their way of life, and imitate their** trust—Yeshua **the Messiah is the same yesterday, today and forever.**"* (Hebrews 13:5–8, CJB, emphasis added)

"Unless Yehovah builds the house, its builders work in vain. Unless Yehovah guards the city, the guard keeps watch in vain. In vain do you get up early and put off going to bed, working hard to earn a living. **For he provides for his beloved, even when they sleep**" (Psalm 127:1–2, CJB, emphasis added).

"Furthermore, **we know that God causes everything to work together for the good of those who love God and are called in accordance with his purpose;** *because those whom he knew in advance, he also determined in advance would be conformed to the pattern of his son, so that he might be the firstborn among many brothers; and those whom he thus determined in advance, he also called; and those whom he called, he also caused to be considered righteous; and those whom he caused to be considered righteous, he also glorified!"* (Romans 8:28–30, CJB, emphasis added)

"My sheep listen to my voice, I recognize them, they follow me and I give them eternal life. **They will absolutely never be destroyed, and no one will snatch them from my hands.** *My Father, who gave them to me, is greater than all; and no one can snatch them from the Father's hands. I and the Father are one"* (John 10:27–30, CJB, emphasis added).

May these pages provide insight, hope, and above all else, a clear trumpet that you are indeed loved, forgiven through the blood and broken body of Yeshua on the cross, and called to live a renewed life through the resurrection power of the Holy Spirit! To God be all the Glory!

—Rose Hammer, Founder/CEO, The Delsa, thedelsa.com
"No one should be alone."

ACKNOWLEDGMENTS

To the many remarkable people who supported this endeavor. Words cannot express my gratitude to all of you. Special thanks to my test readers and advisors for your love, support, and invaluable feedback—I truly could not have done this without you! I love you, all.

Kyle Crouso—those several times you spoke God's wisdom though I didn't believe it at first. Grateful for friendships rekindled!

Jennifer Franko—your single question that changed the course of this entire effort: "Are you sure you're still writing a memoir?" God used you in the most pivotal way!

Rose Hammer—your prayers, belief in me, and willingness to challenge me along the way were some of the greatest gifts I was given for this project. You are a true reflection of our Lord!

Sharmaine Pechec—your willingness to be the listening ear as I processed the reality that God had changed the course of my book. Your encouragement was life when I needed it!

Holly Penhorwood—my soul sister whose consistent and *plentiful* reminders of God's grace were fuel for my soul.

You have always believed in me more than I have believed in myself—and you are a significant reason this project made it to the finish line!

April Vanover—one of the most faithful Sisters I have! Your genuine and abundant encouragement, coupled with spiritual insight, were oxygen on God's flame within me!

Jessica Villa-Cruz—one of my greatest cheerleaders! I can always count on you to calm the voices in my mind and remind me of what is possible.

A special callout to fellow-authors Kati Kleber (author of *Becoming Nursey, The Nurse's Guide to Blogging, Anatomy of a Super Nurse, What's Next? The Smart Nurse's Guide to Your Dream Job, Admit One: What You Must Know When Going to the Hospital,* and *Pediatrics Nclex Essentials: A Nursing School Guide*) and Renee Vidor (author of *Measuring Up: How to Win in a World of Comparison*). I can never repay you for all you have given. You are what the world needs. *Thank you!*

To Author Academy Elite and Igniting Souls Publishing for the incredible community, resources, and unique model that allows authors to achieve their dreams of writing a book!

Above all, I give thanks to my Heavenly Father, the God of Abraham, Isaac, and Jacob, and of my Savior, Jesus Christ. By your grace, I am here today to carry out your will. Thank you for your continued long-suffering, guidance, and, most importantly, grace. All glory to you.

INTRODUCTION

I am very accustomed to people calling me "driven," an "over-achiever," "Type A," and a "perfectionist"—always with an undertone of "weirdo" or "nut case." I would balk at them, sometimes quietly, but often mocking them. Sometimes I simply denied it to their faces. After all, they didn't know what they were talking about.

"I just have higher standards than they do," I would tell myself. "So what if I appreciate getting things done and done well? What's the problem?"

What they defined as over-the-top, I saw as having a higher appreciation for excellence than most. I couldn't understand why they weren't hungrier to do more with their lives or be better at everything they put their hands to. As far as I was concerned, *they* were the abnormal ones!

And then God began to show up. Little by little, He pointed to my anxiety and exhaustion, revealing to me that they were, in fact, the result of my own striving to be perfect. My eyes began to open, and I started to see what everyone else had been seeing for years. It was true; I was a perfectionist.

Soon I was on a journey from self-imposed bondage to freedom I had not known before, a journey to a place where peace prevails and hope rises, where my insides are more at rest.

Don't get me wrong; I haven't totally recovered from my perfectionism. That's why I call it a journey. But I am more confident that the person I am on the inside matches what others see on the outside. And I find it easier to believe that I am enough, just as I am. Before, I tried to align with my own ideal; now, my heart has become aligned with the heart of God. I believe you can also take this journey and experience this freedom and peace.

* * *

Experienced Christians will likely be most comfortable with some of the language and concepts in this book, but I encourage you to continue reading regardless of where you are on your faith journey. God's Spirit can reveal the secrets of His heart to anyone.

If you feel a strong urge to say, "This isn't for me. There's nothing wrong with me," I've got news for you. You may be a perfectionist; keep reading! If, on the other hand, you aren't quite sure, but you have a strong sense that this book may be good for you, trust yourself and keep reading! Or maybe you know you are a hot mess, and you picked this book up, hoping that something in these pages is the medicine you are looking for. Read on!

I trust you are where you need to be. My prayer is that God's Spirit touches you in ways that only He can and that you will, as it says in Ephesians 1:18–19, "*. . . know and understand the hope to which He has called you, and how rich is His glorious inheritance in the saints (His set-apart ones), and [so that you can know and understand] what is the immeasurable and unlimited and surpassing greatness of His power in and for us who believe, as demonstrated in the working of His mighty strength . . .*" (AMPC).

Journey with me as we embark on finding God's grace in the midst of perfectionism.

PART 1

THE RULES

1

PRISONER OF PERFECTIONISM

Years of Bondage

I don't like mistakes—at least not when I am the one making them. I can easily overlook others' mistakes, but I have a much harder time when I am the one at fault. The irritation I feel at my own missteps isn't a simple annoyance that gnaws at me for a few minutes before I can let it go. It's a full-on assault of accusing and condemning internal voices that replay my mistakes and relentlessly remind me of what a failure I am.

Maybe you hear those voices too. If so, you know they may last for days or even years until they become your closest companions, always pushing you to be perfect.

Over time, they grow like vines in the garden of your soul until your entire belief system is rooted in the lie that you are not good enough unless you reach perfection. Your life becomes a series of criticisms that grow together like merciless weeds around your mind until you're consumed with depression, anxiety, and a host of other barriers to peace. The louder the voices are, the more you strive.

Even worse, you carry the same destructive beliefs into your Christian faith, leaving you burned out and robbed of joy and intimacy with Him.

Sound familiar?

UNDERSTANDING PERFECTIONISM

One definition of perfectionism is:

"A broad personality style characterized by a person's concern with striving for flawlessness and perfection and is accompanied by critical self-evaluations and concerns regarding others' evaluations."[1]

Gordon Flett and Paul Hewitt, two leading authorities in the field of perfectionism, say that perfectionists are known for having "unrealistic expectations and thinking or feeling negatively when those expectations aren't being met."[2]

Flett and Hewitt published a landmark study almost three decades ago that suggests three different facets of perfectionism:

1. Self-oriented perfectionism—expecting yourself to be perfect
2. Other-oriented perfectionism—expecting others to be perfect
3. Socially prescribed perfectionism—believing that others expect you to be perfect[3]

They argue that *everyone* struggles, to some degree or another, with one or a mix of these aspects of perfectionism. My biggest struggle has been the self-oriented kind, which you will hear more about as you read on.

Many factors can cause perfectionism, ranging from inborn tendencies to environmental ones, such as excessive demands of a parent or modeling a parent's behaviors. It can be difficult to identify the cause because every person is unique. The effects of perfectionism, regardless of its source, can damage one's mental and physical health, resulting in extreme anxiety and stress, constant self-condemnation, oppression and depression, various addictions, or even suicide.

Signs of perfectionism can include:

- You want to be the best in everything you do.
- You have very high expectations for yourself and others.
- You are very upset with yourself if you make a mistake.
- You feel guilty for relaxing. You feel like you are never doing enough.
- You're very particular about the details of tasks.
- When you perform well, you analyze your performance for the weak spots and quickly gloss over the things done right.
- You want something done right or not done at all.
- You are perceived by others as a role model.
- You feel like others are never satisfied by your performance.
- You compare yourself to others. If you perceive someone is better than you, you analyze that person to see how to measure up.
- You don't attempt things you know you can't complete with excellence.
- You are frightened by the thought of failure.
- You procrastinate.
- Your relationships can be strained or difficult.
- You feel like you won't ever be perfect.
- You rarely experience joy.
- You constantly focus on the destination.[4]

I struggle with one or more of these on a daily basis.

You may be thinking, How could being "perceived as a role model" or being "particular about the details of a task" be bad? Some of the items on this list seem good and even godly! You are not wrong.

Certain behaviors may be good in themselves, but with perfectionism, the problem lies in the motive behind the behaviors. As you will learn, at the heart of perfectionism is a wounded and prideful heart that replaces God's ways with man's and is the greatest barrier to the life He desires to bring you.

THE AWAKENING

To give you an idea of how perfectionism took root and evolved in my life, let me take you on a little journey back in time.

I was eight years old when I began journaling. I'm not sure what prompted me to start; I was a creative being, so stories and poems were a natural draw for me. I also needed to express myself outwardly, and journaling provided a safe environment to sort things out without keeping everything bottled up inside. There was something about journaling that made it possible to survive. Over the years, I accumulated volume after volume of my life experiences and deepest secrets. Rarely did I revisit my journals, though it felt important to have them close by for some unknown reason. One day, that changed.

I was in my late twenties when my life took a radical turn. To the world, I appeared successful, and I was perceived as having it all together. Deep inside me, however, was a little girl whose heart and mind held unhealthy beliefs that led her down tracks of destruction in an attempt to validate her self-worth.

I had been a Christian for a few years, and in a very short time, I had dated one man, been engaged to another, gone through a breakup, and become engaged to yet another man. My life seemed to be operating at warp speed. Even so, I was completely unaware that something was off.

One morning, I awoke in a deep state of fear. My heart was pounding rapidly, and panic ran through my veins. I liken it to the feeling that happens when you are about to have a head-on collision with another vehicle but somehow avoid an actual accident. Adrenaline and fear race through your body, but eventually, you realize you are okay, and things calm down.

In this case, however, I was unaware of where the panic was coming from, so I didn't know if I was okay and could not get settled. The fear and panic cycled for three days, during which I did not sleep, I lost almost ten pounds, and I wound up in the emergency room.

A dark period followed. My senses were extremely heightened. The slightest sound felt jarring; I could feel the very vibrations throughout my entire body. A storm had risen inside that threw me every which way with no time to breathe. I was drowning in despair, full of confusion, fear, and every other emotion under the sun. I could see the concern and worry on the faces of the ones I loved, and the anguish inside my heart grew worse the more helpless they all felt. Something was happening, but nobody knew what it was. Time stood still as I faced the unknown that was before me.

And then God showed up. I was introduced to a relative of an ex-boyfriend who had experienced a similar thing. She was a godsend. Before long, I received a large envelope from her with a book and a handwritten letter. As I read every word, hope began to arise within. For the first time in weeks, somebody was putting into words exactly what I had been experiencing! The diagnosis? An acute nervous breakdown (later confirmed by the doctors).

From a physiological standpoint, my body had created so much adrenaline that my nerves could not handle it, and they broke just like a bone. This phenomenon is known as the fear-adrenaline-fear cycle. It starts with fear, which creates a rush of adrenaline. Because the source of the fear is unknown, it creates more fear, which creates more adrenaline. Eventually, the body cannot handle it, resulting in a nervous breakdown.

God had my attention. Unbeknownst to me, there were things in my life that needed to be addressed, but the only way for me to realize it was through a dramatic awakening like this. My body had to force me to pause long enough to consider what needed to change.

* * *

As with any traumatic experience, healing takes time. My case was extreme enough that I had to go on medical leave from work, move in with friends so that I had 24/7 support, start immediate therapy with a counselor, and begin small doses of drugs to bring balance to the imbalance within me.

It was then that I began revisiting my journals with the hope that I would find answers to what led to the breakdown. Though my body experienced acute physical symptoms, I believed they were the result of something much deeper. I wanted answers.

EARLY BLOOMER

I came across my first diary from when I was seven years old. I smiled as I reminisced. Each entry mostly captured the daily events of life, such as what activities I did that day or where I went and with whom. For the most part, my diary didn't contain any earth-shattering content that would make it to the bestseller list anytime soon. But that was okay; it had been my confidante, I held its key, and that was all that mattered.

As I entered third and fourth grade, there were times when deeper thoughts were expressed in my journal, like whom I had a crush on that day or what I thought of myself.

Sadly, my entries began to be filled with sadness, anger, self-loathing, and depression. I was still very young, but statements like, "I wish I weren't so fat," or "I hate so-and-so," filled many pages. I constantly compared myself to others, especially the skinny girls, always wishing I looked like them. Unbeknownst to me, perfectionism had begun taking root in the garden of my soul, shaping my view of myself and my response to life. (Unfortunately, this carried into adulthood.)

During that same season, my family had just moved to the little town of Hilliard, Ohio, where my siblings and I were enrolled in a local Catholic elementary school. Catholicism was central to my Italian heritage and was where I was first introduced to God. My parents attended Catholic schools as children, and my mother held her faith close to her heart. It was very important to her that we attend church as a family.

I consistently made the honor roll and was invited into advanced math classes at one point because I was accelerating and doing so well. I joined the basketball team and was a leading scorer. Then I got into softball. Life was fun.

Then things began to change. Little by little, the bullying started. I'll call them Beth and Sally. They were the bigwigs in our class. Beth was the ringleader, while Sally was her right-hand woman. Whatever they said was how things were going to be. Each week, Beth and Sally would choose who they would allow in and who would be out. I can't recall exactly when these dynamics began, but I can sure remember wishing so badly that I would be chosen. Instead, I became more and more ostracized, as if there was a special target on my back.

What started as a weekly cycle turned into two and three weeks of being alone. Then it grew into not being invited to birthday parties and people not showing up to mine. We were a small class, so everyone knew what was going on, and there weren't many people left to be friends with after Beth and Sally had their say.

The worst memory was when I found a note on the playground with bad things written about me. It crushed me to have others reject me so deeply. I had a few friends outside Beth and Sally's group, but this rejection still haunted me and had a major impact on my self-esteem. What started as "I wish I weren't so fat" became, "There must be something so wrong with me that is causing them not to like me," and "I am a horrible person and must not be good enough."

As a child, I was not equipped to discern that what was happening to me was abnormal; therefore, I found no reason to run to the adults in my life to discuss it or to seek help. I have no doubt they would have wanted to help me, but for some reason, it was not a natural response. Children often internalize their thoughts and feelings, drawing unhealthy conclusions about what is true. This was my reality, anyway, and by the age of ten, my brain had been hardwired to believe that something was wrong with me and that to avoid any rejection, I would need to figure out exactly how to perform. Whenever I was rejected, I concluded that I must not have performed perfectly; after all, had I done so, I wouldn't have been rejected, right?

KEEPING UP APPEARANCES

Fast forward to the early 90s, and I was fresh out of high school. The love of my life had just dumped me for someone else, and the sting of rejection still haunted me. I already believed that I was fat and ugly, so this new season of my life only reinforced the idea that I must not have been pretty enough or skinny enough to keep my boyfriend. I simply concluded that I was not good enough. (It just keeps growing, doesn't it?)

From there, I began a journey to improve my physical appearance. Exercise became a priority above all things, and I invested in weightlifting and cardio daily. I cut calories to unhealthy levels. Every single day I studied myself in the mirror, critiquing every ounce of my body that I felt was too big, wide, thick, or ugly. I spent hours doing my hair, making sure every strand was right where it was supposed to be. I entered each day as if I were dressing to perform on stage; I ended each day full of pressure to get up and do it all over again, all while juggling a job, college, and social life. To the outsider, I was succeeding at all I put my hands to. On the inside, perfectionism continued to suffocate me like weeds in a garden, causing extreme expectations of myself and anxiety and stress when I couldn't live up to them.

By the time I had entered my mid-twenties, the not-good-enough belief system was so deeply rooted in me that it impacted every decision I made. I continued to have failed relationships with men, mainly because I didn't believe I was worth anything. I either picked men who were very unhealthy, or I felt too inadequate for the good ones, so I never gave them a real chance, though more than anything, I longed to love and be loved.

In my work life, I continued outperforming many of my peers, resulting in promotion after promotion. One day, I found myself in britches too big for my skill set, yet afraid to admit it to anyone. Determined to succeed, I suffered in silence while living with high levels of anxiety and fear on a daily basis. I constantly felt as if I had no idea what I was doing yet assumed I had to figure it out on my own. To admit my weaknesses would make me look bad in the eyes of my authorities. I strived even more to ensure I would not fail, and as usual, the rest of the world saw me performing at or above expectations. (Do you see the signs in my life?)

By day I managed to portray that all was well in my world. Meanwhile, several nights a week, I was out drinking and partying to help drown the noise and pain within. Some may even say I was a high-bottom addict. I started attending AA meetings to fix whatever was happening inside of me, but nothing seemed to stick, and every day, I felt as though my insides were screaming so loudly that my body would implode. My health grew increasingly worse, and at one point, I was getting strep throat and sinus infections about once per quarter as my immune system failed to keep up. It was then that I knew there was no other place to turn but to God. He was the path I previously flirted with but now believed was my only way to real peace.

I dialed Janine, a long-time girlfriend who had left the party scene, found Jesus, and married her high school sweetheart. In my self-destructive mode, I had hurt her, but she met me with open arms and unconditional love. She and her pastor's wife guided me through Scripture as I sought new answers to the pain within. It all brought such hope and excitement to me that on October 16, 1994, I surrendered my heart, declared my commitment to Jesus, and was baptized.

Looking back, I can't say I understood all that was happening. The doctrine I was taught placed great emphasis on water baptism, and most of what I understood was that I needed to be baptized to be saved from the consequence of sin and eternal damnation. I couldn't tell you what the "Blood of Christ" meant or what His death did for me; I barely knew what water baptism meant. What I can tell you, years later, knowing God as I know Him today, is that He honored my heart. The very little I did know, I acted on with sincerity and a true desire to be right with Him. Because of that, He lovingly accepted me into the Kingdom.

So that's it, right? All was now well, my sins were washed clean, and I was a whole new creature. *Perfection!* Except you and I both know it doesn't work like that. Salvation was just the beginning.

* * *

In my humble opinion, one of the greatest pitfalls when introducing people to the Christian faith is to spend too little time teaching the basics about having a relationship with Jesus, why He exists, and what His death and resurrection actually do for us. More often than not, we jump to the "how-to-become-a-Christian" in our hunger to see another soul adopted into the eternal kingdom, and the next thing you know, there are twenty more souls saved, and we're off to the closest body of water we can find to baptize them. Precious motive, not-so-great method. We forge ahead, teaching from Scripture, using all kinds of Christian language, and feeding them advanced knowledge when it's likely they couldn't tell you what the Blood of Jesus even means, let alone what grace is. It's important to be intentional about teaching certain basics, combined with mentorship.

Overemphasizing what to do and how to do it versus *why* we need to do it can be a brooding ground for perfectionism. Remember, perfectionists love formulas; the more we follow the rules, the more we can achieve, and the more valuable we feel. When I am in rule mode, I am often not even challenging the reasons I am doing it; I am just getting things done.

For a time after my baptism, my heart was full of joy, but it didn't take long for me to define my relationship with the Lord as something to be earned. My years of practice as

13

a perfectionist equipped me to apply the same beliefs and approach to my spiritual walk.

As with everything in my life, I went all in (perfectionism, check!). I attended church once on Wednesday and twice on Sunday. I invested in daily Scripture study and prayer, and fasting became a regular exercise for me. I learned the "thou shalt's" and the "thou shalt nots" and the necessity of maintaining righteous living if God was ever going to hear my prayers. I stopped drinking, cussing, and partying of any kind; I even got rid of CDs containing non-Christian music. I made sure I dressed appropriately and did my best to act as a Christian should.

The more I obeyed, the better I felt about myself, and the more I believed I was pleasing the Lord. I was full of the desire to follow Jesus until death, no matter the cost. The Bible became my playbook for success, and nothing made me happier than to follow its hundreds of rules!

You get the picture.

Eventually, I began to wear out mentally and physically. The pattern typically went something like this: If I committed a sin, then I would mentally spiral into condemnation and spend the next few days beating myself up and avoiding God because of the fear of His punishment. Usually, about the third day, I would crawl my way back to Him in prayer, hoping He had forgiven me. If I committed the same sin again soon after, the condemnation would be much harder. I would add a few more "I'm sorrys," some extra Bible time, and the most perfect behaviors I could muster until the pattern would repeat itself. But no amount of work I did was ever going to be enough. We perfectionists can never really reach the standards we set for ourselves because those standards are always on the horizon and can never be reached.

Perfectionism has been bondage, and I have been its prisoner.

The older I have gotten, the harder it has been to maintain the pace and effort I put forth from the start. I was twenty-four when I became a Christian; I am fifty as I write this book. Much has happened in the many years I have walked with the Lord, most of which has been Him unraveling the misconceptions I have had about who He is and what it means to be a Christian.

Maybe you have had a similar experience. It's okay. Grace is real and available now; otherwise, Jesus died in vain. So, stay with me. The light of day is coming.

2

IS IT CHRISTIAN TO BE A PERFECTIONIST?

The Law as a Tutor

Christians are likely to react to perfectionism in two ways. The Christian perfectionist will think, *Shouldn't I desire to be perfect as my father in Heaven is perfect? That's the whole point, isn't it?* Meanwhile, Christians who don't struggle with perfectionism may look at perfectionists and think, *They must not know God as well as they think if they think it's all about the rules.*

If you've thought either of those things, I'm here to tell you it's more complicated than both of them—the rules and grace work hand in hand.

Earlier I stated that my first years with the Lord were not built upon a strong understanding of what Jesus did for me and why; in other words, those years were not built upon a foundation of God's grace. My hope is to equip you with key principles about grace so you can have a more solid understanding of what it is and how to tap into it.

* * *

You may be wondering about the fact that God Himself requires rules to be followed. Isn't that a biblical principle? Didn't God establish the Ten Commandments? Aren't those the first ten rules given to the Jewish people that set the foundation for their ethics, behavior, and responsibility? And aren't there another six hundred laws (603 to be exact) as laid out in the Pentateuch (also known as the Law of Moses, the Mosaic Law, or the Law), that are the moral code by which they were to live and be able to have fellowship with God? Isn't the entire foundation of Christianity built upon following rules *in order to be accepted* by God?

In other words, isn't it Christian to seek perfection?

The answer is yes—sort of. If you stop there, you miss the deeper truths hidden behind the Law and, ultimately, the heart of God. In other words, it is very important first to understand *why* the Law was established so that you can understand its *purpose*. When you understand purpose, you understand motive, and when you understand motive, you can more easily understand the nature, character, and heart of the One who established it.

So, what is the purpose of the Mosaic Law?

In other words, the Law is a means to an end.

For mankind to be ready for Jesus, they would first have to learn certain principles, namely, how to live morally and ethically, how to treat others, how to honor God, and the idea

> **"THE LAW WAS OUR SCHOOLMASTER TO BRING US UNTO CHRIST . . ."**
> —GALATIANS 3:24, KJV

that choices lead to consequences, both good and bad. They were being taught the principles of living a disciplined lifestyle and the practice of sacrificing on a regular basis in order to restore fellowship with God. They were learning obedience. Establishing the Law allowed mankind to begin to understand *sin,* its consequences, and ultimately what would be the solution for it. Without it, man would not have known what sin is, let alone the fact that they would need a solution for it.

In the words of the Apostle Paul:

> What then do we conclude? Is the Law identical with sin? Certainly not! Nevertheless, *if it had not been for the Law, I should not have recognized sin or have known its meaning.* [For instance] I would not have known about covetousness [would have had no consciousness of sin or sense of guilt] if the Law had not [repeatedly] said, You shall not covet and have an evil desire [for one thing and another].
>
> —Romans 7:7, AMPC

So, we see that God was establishing some things in man that would prepare him for the coming of Jesus.

There's another point regarding the Law. God was setting the foundation for what I believe is most important to Him above all else—*relationship.*

To be in a relationship means to be connected through something more than just what is on the surface. It's something deep within the heart and soul of individuals that shapes how they interact with one another.

God desires to be connected to His people intimately, just as you are connected with someone you love here on earth—even more so. He desires to share His heart and the many riches of His kingdom. He desires to commune with His children, listening to their joys and tears, hopes and fears while providing comfort, guidance, and counsel. He desires to interact with each child on a very personal basis, just as you would your closest companion. It is easy to miss God's heart within the Law if you merely see it as a set of rules to be followed.

With more than six hundred commandments, it's notable that Jesus said the greatest commandment of all emphasizes relationship.

"TEACHER, WHICH IS THE GREAT COMMANDMENT IN THE LAW? AND HE SAID UNTO HIM, THOU SHALT LOVE THE LORD THY GOD WITH ALL THY HEART, AND WITH ALL THY SOUL, AND WITH ALL THY MIND. THIS IS THE GREAT AND FIRST COMMANDMENT. AND A SECOND LIKE UNTO IT IS THIS, THOU SHALT LOVE THY NEIGHBOR AS THYSELF."

—MATTHEW 22:36–39, ASV

You only need to read through the Old Testament to see how every command inherently had the essence of relationship at the heart of it. Think about it. Already in the Ten Commandments, He is establishing that principle.[5] In the first four, relationship with Him is the priority:

1. No other gods
2. No idols
3. God's name
4. Keep Sabbath holy

Then in the last six, relationship with others is the priority:

5. Honor parents
6. Do not murder
7. Do not commit adultery
8. Do not steal
9. Do not give false testimony
10. Do not covet

Obedience to God's commands, *from a genuine heart of faith*, is just the beginning. Obedience is essential to entering into a relationship with Jesus and maintaining a connection with Him. It is also how He knows we love Him.

God was never going to remove our responsibility to obey and do our part; He also knew we were never going to be able to do our part *perfectly*, which is why He set up a way to pay for man's imperfections. This is key to understanding the difference between God's grace and what is at the heart of perfectionism.

> **"IF YOU LOVE ME, YOU WILL KEEP MY COMMANDMENTS."**
>
> —JOHN 14:15, NASB

Our biblical translations can sometimes lead us into error without intending to. For instance, when God said, "Thou shalt be *perfect* with the Lord thy God" (Deuteronomy 18:13, KJV), He was using the Hebrew word *tāmîm*, which means several things: complete, wholesome, healthful, sound, unimpaired, innocent, having integrity, entirely in accord with truth and fact.[6] In essence, God was asking them to follow Him *with their whole heart*, as purely as they could, with the right intentions, and He would preserve and bless all they put their hands to. He was not saying never to make a mistake lest He disown them as His children.

Perfectionists struggle to accept this fact. We have a hard time believing that we cannot achieve or *are not required* to meet the standards of the Law perfectly. We do not want to accept that payment has to be made for our mistakes because we ultimately believe we are more valuable and lovable if we pay the price ourselves.

At the very root of my belief system has been the idea that I am not worth anything unless I perform to a particular standard, and somewhere deep inside, I have believed that God believes the same. With that as my driving force, I set out on a mission to perform for Him using my own strength, even if it killed me.

As you can see, motive matters. Where is your heart? What is causing you to pursue perfection? What belief is driving you? Do you believe walking perfectly after God means you are expected not to make mistakes? Or do you understand that He is looking for your heart to be all in?

Be careful not to confuse perfectionism with obedience from a perfect heart. While they may look similar on the outside, the issue is what's within. We will get into this in greater detail.

3

PRINCIPALITIES OF
PERFECTIONISM

What is really behind your bondage?

A nother important point needs to be made before we move on to grace: This is a spiritual world.

For many Christians, walking with Jesus never goes beyond the natural realm, beyond what can be obtained through the senses of touch, taste, smell, sight, and hearing. Some might mentally agree with Scripture that speaks of spiritual things such as angels and demons, but to apply such truths personally is beyond their comprehension. It is one of the greatest detriments to the Christian walk.

Followers of Jesus understand that a spiritual world encompasses the physical one we live in. Inherent to our faith are some key beliefs:

1. There are places called Heaven and Hell,[7] in one of which every human will spend eternity based on their choices.
2. Before man was created, an angel (traditionally known as Satan) rebelled against God and was cast out of Heaven along with other fallen angels.[8]

3. Satan's entire mission, along with his army, is to keep as many people from Heaven as possible. Scripture says that he "prowls around like a roaring lion [fiercely hungry], seeking someone to devour" (1 Peter 5:8, AMP) and that he comes to "steal and kill and destroy" (John 10:10, ASV).

The point is that there are unseen forces whose sole purpose is to influence you in whatever way necessary to keep you from living the life of peace, joy, and freedom that God intended for you. Ultimately, their job is to ensure you do not discover what is possible through a healthy relationship with

> **"FOR WE DO NOT WRESTLE AGAINST FLESH AND BLOOD, BUT AGAINST PRINCIPALITIES, AGAINST POWERS, AGAINST RULERS OF THE DARKNESS OF THIS AGE, AGAINST SPIRITUAL HOSTS OF WICKEDNESS IN THE HEAVENLY PLACES."**
> —EPHESIANS 6:12, NKJV

Jesus. If they can stop you from an intimate relationship with Jesus, they can also stop you from fulfilling your destiny and impacting others toward the same.

These spiritual forces have influenced your life and the lives of those around you, and the source of them is demonic. I am not speaking of demonic possession as is found in Scripture such as Matthew 12:43–45 or Mark 9:17–29; that topic is outside the scope of this book. I'm speaking of the effect on your character, development, or behavior due to demonic sources.

The spiritual realm doesn't just contain evil forces. In Luke 1:15–17, an angel of the Lord tells Zacharias that his unborn son, John the Baptist, would "be filled with the Holy Ghost, even from his mother's womb." (ESV) This example is filled with spiritual influence:

"And he [John the Baptist] will go before him [Jesus] *in the spirit and power of Elijah,* to turn the hearts of the fathers to the children, and the disobedient to the wisdom of the just, to make ready for the Lord a people prepared." (ESV)

Zacharias was conversing with a spiritual being (an angel) who was speaking about his unborn son, John the Baptist, who was to precede the coming of Jesus and would walk in the spirit and power of a man who was no longer alive! Elijah was a prophet who stood against the prophets of Baal and the wickedness in Israel during his time. John the Baptist would be given a similar power to Elijah to carry out the mission God had ordained for him.

If you accept some Scripture, you must accept all of it. It's a spiritual world.

This principle is key to overcoming perfectionism; it means that there are outside forces that have influenced your belief system and behaviors. In the Christian realm, this spirit is often referred to as a religious spirit. It convinces you that following a system of rules makes you holy and acceptable. It seeks for its victims to conduct acts of obedience out of obligation or to earn acceptance. Sound familiar? Remember the Law that was required of the Israelites? As we saw, it was intended to be a tutor that would lead people to a relationship with the Lord with the hope that their obedience would flow from that relationship as opposed to obeying to earn His acceptance. The latter is religion, not relationship; it is a counterfeit spirit the demonic realm wants to create to have dominion over you.

The Pharisees and Sadducees were notorious for operating from a religious spirit. They placed great emphasis on following the Law and making themselves look spiritual, yet their hearts were far from God. When Jesus finally came, many of them could not receive Him because their hearts were so full of pride that they didn't even recognize Him.

Curt Landry of Curt Landry Ministries says it well when he defines a religious spirit as "a type of demonic spirit that influences a person, or group of people, to replace a genuine relationship with God with works and traditions. When people operate out of a religious spirit, they attempt to earn salvation."

He says, "it [religious spirit] often uses a person's history and circumstances to afflict internal whispers of judgment and pressure to perform. These infectious lies plant seeds of false righteousness and holiness."[9]

I couldn't have said it better myself.

* * *

Remember that journal I found with unhealthy belief systems already forming? Spiritual influences had already begun a work in my life. Those girls who bullied me in elementary school? Satan's army was behind that too.

The garden of perfectionism within me had formed fruit, one of which was the belief that everything was my fault. It took me years to accept that something else, or someone else, may be responsible for influencing my behaviors. Don't get me wrong, I am not suggesting that you or I don't play a part in our actions; we are ultimately responsible for the choices we make. No one forced me to pick up the alcohol I chose to self-medicate with. But to allow someone else to take some responsibility for influencing my choices meant removing me from my opportunity to perform to a certain standard so that I could be found acceptable.

In the situation involving the bullies at school, it never crossed my mind that their actions were inappropriate (it sounds so crazy to say that now!). To this day, when an accusation is brought against me, I must be slow and intentional in evaluating it before drawing any conclusions. I am not as quick to conclude everything really is my fault, but I still have to work at it.

This conflict can be a normal part of the journey for a perfectionist. To embrace the new reality is empowering; it allows you to understand that there is a spiritual battle where one force desires to lead you to life and the other to death. You get to choose which path you want to partner with.

Satan and his army are very schooled in spiritual matters and already know what Scripture says. They know how to masquerade themselves to make you think something is of God when it's really a counterfeit or to make you think there is some other source of the cause than them. They watch you, me, and generations before us to learn how we operate. Then they develop strategies to attack through demons, other people, circumstances, and anything else they can find. Studies show that a baby's emotional and cognitive development begins around six months in the womb, so it's possible for the demonic realm to attack even before a baby is born. Then he spends the rest of the child's life attempting to keep him or her from God's truth.

Are you seeing it? Every day you awake to a list of all of the things you need to accomplish that day. As the day goes on, you are acutely aware of every action you take, your mind constantly assessing and grading the quality of your work, and if your work is good and aligned with what a Christian *should* do, you are at peace and happy with yourself. If the opposite is true, you may end up in despair, anger, shame, and resentment, among other things. Your mind is constantly on, your insides constantly in motion, every moment of every day. It is utterly exhausting and not sustainable, and every bit of it started from the influence of a religious spirit in your life.

The good news is that God knew this would be the case from the beginning, so He had ready the antidote in Jesus. He alone is the answer to our problem, and it is in Him that we find the grace that will set our hearts free from this bondage.

PART 2

THE REMEDY

4

THE LAW OF LIFE—GRACE UNMERITED

The Remedy for Sin

"For the law of the Spirit of life in Christ Jesus hath made me free from the law of sin and death. For what the law could not do, in that it was weak through the flesh, God sending his own Son in the likeness of sinful flesh, and for sin, condemned sin in the flesh."

—Romans 8: 2,3 KJV

While the Law taught many things, including what sin is, it is weak and could not set you and me free from the consequence of sin. If the "wages of sin is death," as Romans 6:23 (KJV) says, then we will always need someone or something to pay the price of sin and death.

You may recall that the Israelites were commanded to conduct certain rituals throughout the year, one of which was to sacrifice lambs to make atonement for sin. These sacrifices were a kind of rehearsal, pointing them to the ultimate sacrifice that would eventually come, namely Jesus, also called the Lamb of God. Jesus's death was the perfect payment for all of mankind's sins; there was no more need for animals to be sacrificed. Jesus became the way for all mankind to be set free from the bondage of sin and from living eternally separate from God. He alone is the gateway to a relationship with the Heavenly Father.

> **"THERE IS NONE OTHER NAME [JESUS] UNDER HEAVEN GIVEN AMONG MEN, WHEREBY WE MUST BE SAVED."**
>
> —ACTS 4:12, KJV

Jesus personally proclaimed, "I am the way, the truth, and the life: *no man cometh unto the Father, but by me*" (John 14:6, KJV).

In the New Testament, the announcement that Jesus brought the reign of God to our world through His life, death, and resurrection from the dead is known as the Gospel of Christ. The word gospel comes from the Greek word *euangelion*, which literally means good news.[10]

It was good news that a Savior had come to save the world from the consequence of sin; this is what "saved by God's grace" means. Mankind would not have to pay the required payment for eternal salvation. The way to salvation could only be achieved through faith in the Blood of Jesus. A new Law was established, the Law of Life, which took precedence over the Mosaic Law. Grace had been established. The Holy Spirit could now live *within* man rather than outside him, replacing man's nature with His. God and man could now become one. I'll touch more on this later.

* * *

Satan wasted no time in creating a counterfeit grace. In keeping with his typical modus operandi, he seduced Christians away from authentic grace. One way he has done this is by reducing the definition of grace to mean an unlimited amount of forgiveness for sin, which leaves the door open for many to think they can sin as they please. The sinner is no longer held accountable for sin nor has to engage in the fight against it. Rather than learning to lean on God's strength and partner with Him to resist the temptations, the sinner simply continues the cycle of sinning, confessing the sin, asking forgiveness, and sinning again; no lasting change in behavior occurs.

Note the following Scripture found in Romans 6 (KJV).

- "What shall we say then? Shall we continue in sin, that grace may abound? God forbid. How shall we, that are dead to sin, live any longer therein ?" (verse 1)

- "Knowing this, that our old man is crucified with him, that the body of sin might be destroyed, that henceforth we should not serve sin." (verse 6)

- "Let not sin therefore reign in your mortal body, that ye should obey it in the lusts thereof." (verse 12)

- "For sin shall not have dominion over you: for ye are not under the law, but under grace." (verse 14)

Grace requires action that leads to repentance or the replacement of a righteous behavior for an unrighteous one.

One of the greatest explanations of grace I have ever read can be found in Dietrich Bonhoeffer's *The Cost of Discipleship*, specifically from the first chapter, "Costly Grace," where he says, "Cheap grace is the deadly enemy of our Church. We are fighting today for costly grace." In essence, he suggests that cheap grace means grace alone does everything and nothing has to change in the sinner. It would be like a church having the principle of grace as its doctrine or system, yet there is no contrition required, no denial of self, and no desire to be delivered from sin.

Costly grace refers to the fact that our salvation cost Jesus His life and should be sought after with our whole hearts.

> **"WHO, WHEN HE HAD FOUND ONE PEARL OF GREAT PRICE, WENT AND SOLD ALL THAT HE HAD, AND BOUGHT IT."**
>
> —MATTHEW 13:46, KJV

Remember the greatest command we referred to in Chapter 2: "Love the Lord your God with all your heart, all your soul, and all your mind"? He was not commanding a half-hearted response. When Jesus called his followers to follow Him, He often told them to drop everything they had and not look back. He was never looking for followers who were lukewarm in their decision to follow Him; He always required a *complete* response that meant a denial of everything.

Martin Luther was a great example of someone who grasped this very thing. After becoming miserable in attempting justification through religious works, he finally "grasped by faith the free and unconditional forgiveness of all his sins. That experience taught him that this grace had cost [Jesus] his very life and must continue to cost him the same price day by day."[11]

Luther understood that he would always face sin in his mortal body. Yet, only Christ's shed blood could cover the cost of that sin, so rather than using grace as an excuse to continue to look like the world, he was instead compelled all the more to follow Jesus with his entire heart, mind, and soul. He grasped the essence that grace justifies the *sinner* as well as the sin, the very thing we must realize if we are truly to walk in grace as He sees it. Cheap grace should be avoided at all costs if we wish to have intimacy with our Savior!

There is good news for the perfectionist in all of this! You get to throw your whole heart into the journey but without the fear of condemnation for making mistakes or the fear of losing your inheritance because you didn't keep up with the requirements. You get to tap into power so strong that it raised Jesus from the dead and now lives in you as the source of strength to help you become more like Jesus, you get to commune with your Creator and learn what is on His heart every step of the way, and you get to walk in joy and freedom you have never known. Are you ready to step into costly grace?

5

COUNTERFEIT CHRISTIANITY

Falling from Grace

You would think it would be easier to respond in faith, knowing that someone paid the price that you and I were meant to pay, than to continue in a system of traditions, rituals, and rules. But that has not been the case throughout the generations since Jesus walked the earth. And as I have discussed, it's important that perfectionists understand the danger that lies ahead and can so easily entangle you into the bondage brought on by the religious spirit.

To best illustrate, let's take a look at the Galatians in the New Testament. These were folks, just like you and me, who had responded to the good news of Jesus with faith and repentance that demonstrated their commitment to living for Him. Then something happened that caused the Apostle Paul to say, "I marvel that you are so soon removed from Him that called you into the grace of Christ unto *another gospel*" (Galatians 1:6, KJV).

Apparently, there had been Judaizers who had entered while Paul was away and deceived the Galatians by teaching them that circumcision and observation of the Law of Moses were required to be saved. In essence, the Judaizers were being influenced by the religious spirit!

Paul went so far as to say this was a perversion of the true Gospel and then proceeded to re-establish the gospel of grace versus law. From the moment he greeted them, he reminded them of the truth: "Grace be to you and peace from God the Father, and from our Lord Jesus Christ, *who gave Himself for our sins*" (1:3–4, KJV). Then he reminded them that even for the Jews, salvation is not earned by their works but by faith in the One who paid the price for them.

Paul reiterates that the death of Jesus took on the demands of the Law for us all. He points back to the fact that we are redeemed, or ransomed, through Christ's death: "*Christ hath redeemed us* from the curse of the Law, being made a curse for us" (3:13, KJV).

> **"WE WHO ARE JEWS BY NATURE . . . KNOWING THAT A MAN IS NOT JUSTIFIED BY THE WORKS OF THE LAW, BUT BY FAITH OF JESUS CHRIST, EVEN WE HAVE BELIEVED IN JESUS CHRIST, THAT WE MIGHT BE JUSTIFIED BY THE FAITH OF CHRIST, AND NOT BY THE WORKS OF THE LAW: FOR BY THE WORKS OF THE LAW SHALL NO FLESH BE JUSTIFIED."**
>
> —GALATIANS 2:16, KJV

Paul spends significant time discussing the inheritance that would come to both Jews and Gentiles through Christ's death and resurrection, establishing that it would come through a promise and not through the Law (which only pertained to Israelites, not Gentiles). He even mentions that those under the Law had to be redeemed so that they may "receive the adoption of sons" (4:5, KJV). He speaks of freedom or liberty that exists through the promise fulfilled in Jesus. He commands the Galatians to "[s]tand fast therefore in the liberty" (5:1, KJV).

He goes so far as to say that those who attempt to live by the Law must live by the whole of it, but that then Christ has "*become of no effect unto you . . . ye are fallen from grace*" (5:4, KJV). We are not talking about losing one's salvation. We are talking about stepping out from under the umbrella of freedom that exists because of what Christ did and stepping back under an umbrella that now requires the person to fulfill the entire law for him or herself. Without realizing it, man shifted from obedience to the Law of Life to obedience to the Law of Sin and Death, resulting in loss of intimacy with Him.

I only need to reflect back to similar times of bondage in my life to see what resulted. If I were to be honest, looking back at my early days of walking with the Lord, there were so many times that I was "puffed up" in my self-righteous thoughts because I believed I was holy based on my ability to follow the Law. Little did I understand the curse I walked in. God began to reveal to me how the religious spirit was influencing my perspectives (the enemy loves nothing more than to imitate the Holy Spirit), leaving me critical of others and full of shame, doubt, and resentment every time I could not live up to its expectations. This is the very bondage Paul spoke of to the Galatians and the revelation Luther experienced.

Remember when I said that one of the most important things God was looking for in the Law was relationships? From the start, God has always emphasized the importance of man's heart being right versus having the appearance of righteousness outwardly while the heart is full of unrighteousness. This concept is often illustrated using the terms "circumcision of the flesh," referring to the natural act of cutting away the flesh, and "circumcision of the heart," a spiritual reference to the cutting away of the hardness of man's heart. Even in the Old Testament, when God required

Abraham and his people to be circumcised at a very old age, it was *after* God had promised Abraham that his descendants would be as the sand on the sea. This is key in that the promise would not come through outer works but by a response of obedience *from a genuine respect for God and a grateful heart.*

From the beginning, God set up a remedy to our sin problem and a way back to a restored relationship with Him. He knew the bondage of sin would always lead to spiritual death and

> **"ALL HAVE SINNED AND COME SHORT OF THE GLORY OF GOD."**
>
> —ROMANS 3:23, KJV

that "there is none righteous, no, not one" (Romans 3:10, KJV).

By His grace—that undeserved thing offered to all—we have a way to be restored and set free from any justification under the Law. Now, anyone and everyone (not just the Israelites or those under the Mosaic law) can be justified by faith.

When we find ourselves bitter, tired, oppressed, or any of the other myriad bad fruits that result from living under the Law, we must check our hearts to see if we have stepped into the counterfeit, repent, and turn back to the One who can set us free.

Can you relate? I certainly can. I have had to be reminded of this time and time again, even now. But the good news is that there is grace for you and me! He understands and stands ready to help you return to the freedom He paid for!

6

GRACE BEYOND

Even More Than We Think

I have established that grace is a kind of favor or gift given to mankind that enables them to be pardoned from the consequence of sin by putting their faith in the work that Jesus already did versus being justified by their own works in following the Law. This is foundational for perfectionists to understand; true freedom starts here.

But grace doesn't stop there; it is so much more than that! (Listen up, you perfectionists. Here's more for your armor belt!) Something happened when the transition from law to grace occurred. Better yet, *someone* happened.

His name is Holy Spirit.

Do you recall what Jesus said to his disciples before he was taken away at Mt. Olivet? He said, "But ye shall receive power, after that the Holy Ghost is come upon you" (Acts 1:8, KJV).

And sure enough, at Pentecost, when they were all gathered in one place, the Holy Spirit came upon them, and they began manifesting signs, wonders, and abilities like had not been before then. This is referred to as the baptism of the Spirit.

Paul later refers to these abilities as "gifts" possible because of God's grace. "Having then gifts differing according to the grace that is given to us" (Romans 12:6, KJV).

* * *

It was sometime around the year 2000. I had just come out of a few years of great turmoil in my life and was on the road to emotional healing. God had led me to a small group of Christians I met weekly for Bible study. We came from similar backgrounds but were hungry for more of God, and as is His nature, He honored us by revealing Himself in ways we could not expect.

I was in a season where my spiritual senses were growing stronger, and I began to recognize God in the details of my life. For many months, He had been speaking to me through a series of events that indicated that He would soon have me quit my job.

Then it happened. I awoke one day with a deep knowledge that I would resign that day. My insides vacillated between fear and faith as adrenaline pushed my body to a near-breaking point. But as scary as the process was, something inside me was absolutely sure it was His will.

I went to work following my usual routine, wondering how things would play out. As I sat in my office checking emails and voicemails, I got a knock on my door. It was my manager. He and I had been discussing my future; I had been identified as a high-potential performer they intended to invest in developing. I had dropped hints that I wasn't sure where I would be.

"I'm here to discuss your development plan. I need a decision from you today," he asserted.

I began to shake internally. I tried to keep it cool on the outside, but inside I was about to freak out.

39

On the one hand, I was amazed at how God had moved my manager to confront me so poignantly on that very morning; the timing was no accident. On the other hand, it was completely illogical to leave a great job with a potentially great future without having another job lined up, all while owning a home for which I was the sole income earner!

"Can I get back to you in a few days?" I asked.

"You either know, or you don't know at this point. A few days won't matter," my manager replied. God was giving me no way out. I would put my trust in the Lord or take the easy way out. My head spun. I sat in silence for what seemed like forever, then I finally asked myself, *Would you regret it if you stayed or regret it if you left?* I knew my answer.

"I'm going to need to resign," I said. And just like that, I was overwhelmed with a peace that I knew was the Lord.

But then something else happened.

A power fell on me, which I now know was the baptism of the Holy Spirit. Suddenly my senses could "see" into spiritual dimensions I had never known! When I looked at people, I had knowledge of things about their lives that I could never have known without the power of God fueling me. I could see things about their future that had not yet happened.

> **"...THE HOLY GHOST CAME ON THEM; AND THEY SPAKE WITH TONGUES, AND PROPHESIED."**
>
> —ACTS 19:6, KJV

Little did I know at that moment that I was moving in the gifts of prophecy and words of knowledge. I didn't know what to think! After all, I had been taught that these gifts were no longer possible and that they ceased many generations ago. Yet, God was opening my spiritual eyes to a whole new world and busting through my religious paradigms. And none of it was possible but by the grace of God.

* * *

By grace, I am saved. By grace, I received the baptism of the Spirit.

Grace brings even more: a power that enables you to walk righteously with the Lord even when you are in distress. You see this in Paul's words in 2 Corinthians 12:9: "And he [Jesus] said unto me, '*My grace is sufficient* for thee: for *my strength is made perfect in weakness.*' Most gladly therefore will I rather glory in my infirmities, *that the power of Christ* may rest upon me" (KJV).

It's grace in the form of power that enabled Paul to keep going.

It's grace as power that enabled the Macedonian churches to give so generously "in the midst of a very severe trial and extreme poverty" (2 Corinthians 8:1–2, KJV).

It's grace as power that enabled Jesus to "taste death for everyone" so you and I would not have to (Hebrews 2:9, KJV).

It's grace as power that enables you and me to overcome sin (Hebrews 4:15–16, KJV).

In the times of the Law, only certain people had access to the Spirit, and that was from the outside. Pentecost was the beginning of the Spirit dwelling *within* believers, only by God's grace.

Having the Holy Spirit within you means that the very power that raised Jesus from the dead now resides inside you, enabling Him to replace your nature with His so that we can help reconcile others to Him, which is the ultimate purpose of our walk with Him. Look what it says in Galatians 2:20: "*I am crucified with Christ*: nevertheless I live; *yet not I, but Christ liveth in me*: and the life which I now live in the flesh I live by the faith of the Son of God, who loved me, and gave himself for me" (KJV).

41

And again, in Romans 8:11: "The Spirit of God, who raised Jesus from the dead, lives in you. And just as God raised Christ Jesus from the dead, He will give life to your mortal bodies by this same Spirit living within you" (KJV).

> **"HOWBEIT WHEN HE, THE SPIRIT OF TRUTH, IS COME, HE WILL GUIDE YOU INTO ALL TRUTH: FOR HE SHALL NOT SPEAK OF HIMSELF; BUT WHATSOEVER HE SHALL HEAR, THAT SHALL HE SPEAK: AND HE WILL SHEW YOU THINGS TO COME."**
>
> —JOHN 16:13, KJV

Even more important than the power that the Holy Spirit ushered in for believers was the fact that every believer now would have direct access to a relationship with the Lord!

How glorious it is to know that anyone who has the Holy Spirit can literally commune with the Lord through His Spirit! This is yet another indication of how God's heart has always pursued a relationship with His children. What a precious thing to think upon.

* * *

There's one other meaning of grace I want to point out, and it is the one that probably touches me the deepest. It comes from a combination of two Hebrew words that mean to show pity or mercy on someone or to find someone acceptable.[12] It's when someone is gracious in their speech or attitude toward another.

Maybe you share the difficulty I have in showing pity or mercy to yourself. As a perfectionist who could never find myself acceptable and who has believed God and others only find me acceptable if I perform to a certain standard, it has been incredibly difficult to accept that it is God's will for me to receive this aspect of grace. I had understood grace to mean that I didn't earn salvation through my works, though I was still in bondage to a religious spirit. But to know God as a gracious father was foreign to me and extremely difficult to receive. Even now, I can easily default to the former way of thinking.

* * *

I'll never forget the season God began to reveal His pity on me. I had been struggling with habitual sin in my life that I could not seem to overcome. As I shared in the first chapter, severe condemnation always followed. To make matters worse, I had lived under a teaching for years that declared a person not really saved if he or she was still stuck in sin, which added fear to the condemnation. I also did not want to abuse God's grace, using it as unlimited forgiveness as other Christians did.

You can imagine my surprise when God showed up one day after I had just failed miserably. I heard Him say, "I am a compassionate Father. I am not here to hurt you." I was utterly shocked.

I could feel tenderness and mercy in His words and immediately felt safe enough to run into His arms and let it all out. Confused yet relieved, I ran to Him, begging for forgiveness, mercy, and strength to overcome. What had been years of white-knuckling my way through temptation turned into a partnership with God to get victory over the habit.

God knew my heart. He knew the reason behind the sin, and He knew that I was not casually engaging in it without any concern for how it would grieve Him. 1 John 4:18 says, "There is no fear in love; but *perfect love casteth out fear*: because fear hath torment. He that feareth is not made perfect in love" (KJV). He knew that more than anything, I needed His perfect love to cast out the fears that drove me to sin in

43

the first place. His perfect love led me straight to His arms and created an even stronger desire to repent.

> ## "THE GOODNESS OF GOD LEADS YOU TO REPENTANCE."
> —ROMANS 2:4, NKJV

It has been incredibly encouraging to know that our Heavenly Father has such compassion and is full of understanding. Joel 2:13 says, "For He is gracious and compassionate, slow to anger, abounding in lovingkindness" (NIV).

I am not suggesting that repentance is not necessary. God has never removed the requirement of repentance from me; however, He placed much more emphasis on introducing me to His heart of mercy and loving-kindness to establish a deeper relationship between us. I expected punishment and anger from Him with each act of disobedience, as if He would disown me and remove my status as His child. Instead, He showed pity and a love that "covers a multitude of sins" (1 Peter 4:8, NIV).

If you discover nothing else reading this book, may you begin to understand that the Creator of the universe understands you like no other, loves you more than you can imagine, and stands ready to reveal His grace and mercy to you as you run to Him. Ultimately, He desires to be in a relationship with you and will pursue that above anything.

PART 3

THE RECIPE FOR FREEDOM

7

THE PROCESS OF PARTNERSHIP

Dancing with Jesus

Now the Lord is the Spirit, and where the Spirit of the Lord is, there is freedom.

—2 Corinthians 3:17, NIV

The above Scripture illustrates God's answer to bondage: *the presence of the Holy Spirit.* In my journey to finding freedom from perfectionism, I have discovered that many recommended solutions place the majority of emphasis on my role in the process, inadvertently suggesting that freedom relies solely on the work I need to do to bring about the change I seek. These solutions often provide lists of behaviors that promise to lead to the intended destination if applied regularly but place little-to-no emphasis on the role that the Holy Spirit plays. This approach has only fed my misguided, performance-based approach, leaving me absent of true transformation.

It isn't that the recommendations are entirely wrong; you and I do play a role in obtaining freedom. However, we are only part of the equation. True freedom is found when we *partner with God* in the process.

LED BY HIS SPIRIT

If it were not for God's Spirit, I would never have known my bondage.

> **"THESE ARE THE THINGS GOD HAS REVEALED TO US BY HIS SPIRIT. THE SPIRIT SEARCHES ALL THINGS, EVEN THE DEEP THINGS OF GOD. FOR WHO KNOWS A PERSON'S THOUGHTS EXCEPT FOR THEIR OWN SPIRIT WITHIN THEM? IN THE SAME WAY, NO ONE KNOWS THE THOUGHTS OF GOD EXCEPT THE SPIRIT OF GOD."**
>
> —1 CORINTHIANS 2:10–11, NIV

It was Christmas 2021, and I was in Florida visiting my father. God had been speaking to me about my book; He had laid it on my heart to pivot from writing a memoir to a book on restoration and recovery. The change threw me for a loop. I had just spent over a year writing the memoir, and now I would need to start all over, which was incredibly overwhelming. I was unaware at the time that I was a perfectionist, and the whole situation was a trigger that sent me spiraling into the bondage of perfectionism.

"What am I supposed to write about?" I exclaimed. "I have no idea what I am doing!" A million thoughts raced through my mind, and my stomach quickly tied up in knots. I became heavily burdened, oppressed, fearful, and overwhelmed, yet I could not get free. My mind raced to fill in the gaps of the unknown with details I didn't have. Perfectionism had gripped me again, and I had stepped completely outside God's grace.

Deep within my spirit, I knew God was separating what was of His Spirit and what was my flesh. I knew the only path forward was to trust and obey, yet all I could see were my inadequacies and fears. I vexed my soul as I wrestled with where I would begin.

As I meditated back to the moment I knew God had called me to write, a couple of things stood out. Back then, I distinctly heard God say, "It's your season; you will make mistakes." I had a strong sense in my spirit that it was Him, and after multiple days of prayer and seeking counsel from several trusted brethren, I received numerous confirmations that further affirmed it was God's call on my life to write a book.

In addition, three different friends independently suggested that God had already provided me with the title of the book when He used the phrase, "you will make mistakes." At the time, I didn't listen because it sounded more like a self-help book than a memoir, and I had already settled on the fact that I was going to write a memoir. When God challenged me toward a new direction, it caused me to revisit the thought; the idea seemed much more fitting.

As I continued meditating on these things, I found myself drawn to the part that said, "you will make mistakes." I wondered if there was significance to that phrase, so I decided to follow that rabbit trail to see where it would lead me. I began Googling things like "perfectionism," "symptoms of perfectionism," and "how to know if you are a perfectionist." I could not believe what I was discovering! Every article I read, every description and symptom, encompassed me. I was staring into the face of my own bondage.

"I never realized that I am a perfectionist!" I exclaimed. Suddenly my life made sense to me, and I knew what the focus of this book would be.

* * *

God had been speaking all along, even through those who suggested my book title. Those signposts were there to guide me into His truth for my life. Even though I did not realize it at first, He allowed me to walk down the path I thought was His until He was ready to reveal a more perfect path. The Holy Spirit led me from the start, leading me into truth the entire time. His Spirit communicated with my Spirit and revealed the mind of God to me. I often like to use the phrase "I know it in my knower" to describe those times when revelation takes place, and experiential knowledge replaces intellectual knowledge; this was one of those times.

You might think that my new revelation brought great pleasure, but symptoms of perfectionism were still present for many months. I toiled over what to write and how to write it; I stressed over what people would think. I felt like Moses, who lacked confidence in his ineloquent speech. (See Exodus 4:10, NIV) and was convinced that God was making a mistake choosing me.

My bondage was in high gear. I stepped out of grace and lost my internal peace. I had a deep sense that my destiny depended on my response to the Lord's call; obedience was my only option. I embraced the new revelation, accepted the road before me, and committed to walking the new path. I could see my bondage and decided I would not remain as I had always been. Eventually, faith began to replace fear, peace grew within, and the words on the page started to flow. The Lord and I were connected once again. The events that exposed my bondage became the catalyst that shaped an even greater measure of freedom in my life.

I still have moments when perfectionism beckons me, but I quickly see it for what it is and run to the Lord for His grace to remain free from bondage.

STAYING CONNECTED

Letting the Holy Spirit lead you into truth is an important first step in overcoming perfectionism and walking in freedom;

however, it is also essential that you learn to *remain* there. This is often referred to as abiding, or in other words, "to tarry or to continue to be present."[13]

Jesus, our leader, is our vine, and we, the followers, are the branches.

Many years ago, I started dance lessons for partner dancing. I had grown up watching my parents dance jitterbug style, and my mom and I used to enjoy watching dance shows such as *Solid Gold* and *Soul Train* as we fantasized about being dancers on set. I couldn't wait to learn so I could become one of them. At the same time I learned to dance, the Lord taught me more about His grace and the leading of His Spirit versus living according to the Law. The timing was no accident.

> "AS THE BRANCH CANNOT BEAR FRUIT OF ITSELF, EXCEPT IT ABIDE IN THE VINE; NO MORE CAN YE, EXCEPT YE ABIDE IN ME. I AM THE VINE, YE ARE THE BRANCHES: HE THAT ABIDETH IN ME, AND I IN HIM, THE SAME BRINGETH FORTH MUCH FRUIT: FOR WITHOUT ME YE CAN DO NOTHING. IF A MAN ABIDE NOT IN ME, HE IS CAST FORTH AS A BRANCH, AND IS WITHERED."
>
> —JOHN 15:5, KJV

I recall my first dance lesson as I stood amongst men and women equally excited to learn. The instructor shared the history of the dance, how it evolved and where it is most popular in the world today. He proceeded to discuss the roles of the man versus the woman, placing special emphasis on the fact that the woman is to *follow*, not lead. The man's job is to make her look beautiful on the dance floor by leading her through a series of movements according to the rhythm of the music.

Suddenly, the Spirit within me revealed the correlation between the dance lesson and the life lesson He was teaching me. Just as I needed to allow the man to lead me through the dance, I needed to learn how to let God's Spirit lead me through life.

One of the most essential elements in partner dancing is what is called a connection. This involves physical, non-verbal communication between both partners to facilitate coordinated movement. The leader must put just the right amount of pressure on the follower's hand, arm, shoulder, or back to communicate to the follower what movement is desired. It could be a spin, a turn, a walk from one side to the other, or even a dip, all of which can be accomplished without words. When both parties maintain the proper connection, the follower can literally dance through a beautiful array of movements simply by listening to the leader's touch and following accordingly. Some of my most impactful dances occurred when I trusted my leader enough to dance with my eyes closed the entire time. Another way of knowing what the leader is communicating is through visual cues, like seeing the leader move in a certain way which would indicate to the follower what is coming.

It's similar to how God speaks to His people. Sometimes you may sense His presence though you do not see Him; other times, you see the evidence of His communication through visual cues in your circumstances or other signs He places in your path. Staying connected to these things allows you to dance to the rhythm of God's song for your life.

On the flip side, you can imagine what happens when the follower either attempts to be the leader or gets distracted and does not pay attention to the leader. The connection breaks, as does the communication between the two. It didn't take me long to learn what can happen when both partners are on two separate wavelengths.

Once, I was enjoying a very upbeat song as I danced with a more experienced dancer. Unfortunately, I was distracted by the music and failed to maintain the connection with my leader. When he went to spin me in one direction, I went in the other direction, which caused my shoulder to be twisted in a way it wasn't intended to go. Thankfully, he was experienced enough to sense it quickly and dropped our connection altogether; however, the sting was strong enough that I have never repeated that mistake since!

There are times in your walk with the Lord when you will experience breaks in your connection with Him. You may experience a situation that stings and causes you to reevaluate whether you are walking in the way of the Lord's will or if you have inadvertently ended up on a different wavelength. This is normal. It does not mean your status as His child changes; it means there is a need to refocus your attention back to His leading and reestablish your connection.

I wish I could say that one example taught me all I needed to know about staying connected to the Lord, but unfortunately, my walk has been full of hard lessons when it comes to this.

* * *

It was the year 2016, and I had just lost my job. The first couple of months were filled with fear and striving (the disconnect begins!) as I searched for something that aligned with my abilities. I was tempted to take any job that could pay the bills and felt more lost than ever as I hit dead ends at every turn. I was grateful when the unemployment checks began arriving, and I could make my house payment.

Throughout the journey, the Lord continued to encourage me to "be still and know" (Psalm 46:10, KJV). How could I be still when I need to pursue? The dance was a difficult one, staying still yet moving forward. It was an internal stillness He was calling me to, a posture of rest and assurance that He would reveal the next step.

Finally, about four months in, I began to rest from the anxiety and worry, live in the moment, and trust in Him. I steadily moved forward, denied the temptation to be anxious, and chose to remain assured and steadfast that the tides would eventually turn in my favor.

"THE STEPS OF THE RIGHTEOUS ARE ORDERED BY THE LORD."

—PSALM 37:23, AMP

The next several months served as a time of great mourning, reflection, and healing. At some point during the waiting, the door opened to travel with my father. Our family had just come through tremendous trials with my father's health, resulting in open-heart surgery and the placement of a device to keep his heart working. It had been a few years since he was able to get away, and I believed sunshine and a change of scenery would be good for him. I prayed and felt peace from the Lord to go. So, in February of 2017, Dad and I went to Florida for a month. We stayed on the coast and thoroughly enjoyed the feel of the sand on our feet and the fresh, salt-water air from the ocean. It was healing for both of us.

One day as I was lounging on the couch, an ad for Match. com popped up. I was never interested in online dating; I had sworn I would never do it. But life had created a desire in me to step out in ways that I wasn't willing to before. As with all decisions like this, I sought the Lord to see what He might say, and I felt released to pursue the dating site. Anxiety filled me throughout, and a million thoughts raced through my mind; it had been so long since I dated. I was flooded by fear of rejection and perfectionism.

Step by step, as best as I knew how, I built a profile that depicted the whole of me. Then I waited.

Within 12 hours, I had 17 hits. I am not sure what I was expecting, but I am reasonably sure it wasn't that. My anxiety rose to a whole new level. There was a point where I finally prayed and asked the Lord to help me relax and enjoy the process. My confidence quickly grew, and one by one, I responded to each of my prospects.

The process was more challenging than I had anticipated. I felt like I spent a huge amount of time rejecting guys, and I soon began to feel overwhelmed and guilty for it. Thankfully, I soon realized I did not need to respond to every inquiry! Eventually, I dwindled the list of potentials from many to a few, and by the time I returned from Florida, I had seven gentlemen lined up and ready to connect. Dad and I joked that these dates would serve as a financial plan during my unemployment!

I can't say any of my first dates were terrible; for the most part, they weren't so bad. I learned that the dating scene was just as challenging for some men as it is for women, but for different reasons. The good guys feel they are mistrusted from the beginning because some men have made a bad name for all men. They talked about the difficulty they face whenever they desire to show interest in a woman, afraid their approach will come off the wrong way. Men worry they will be viewed as having ulterior motives. Others spoke of women who were actually more like predators, often texting nude pictures of themselves after the first date or, worse yet, soliciting sex. It all was a bit shocking, to say the least. I had a whole new appreciation for men and what they go through.

After a round of second dates, my seven became three, but there was one, in particular, that would become one of the most defining relationships in my life.

I had seen pictures of Rob pop up several times, and each time I couldn't decide if I was attracted to him or not. There wasn't much written in his profile, but I was drawn to a picture of him holding his grandson's hand as they walked beside each other. It seemed sweet and was enough to pull on my heartstrings.

Rob initiated contact with a "like" of my profile, and eventually, I responded. Our first date was set for March 20, 2017. I remember it well. Rob worked the night shift as a truck driver, so we planned on a lunch date at Applebee's. Rob attempted to play a joke on me from the start by suggesting the restaurant was closed though he was hiding behind the lobby door. His childlike ways made an odd first impression, though I gradually grew fond of them. Lucky for him, I was in the habit of giving things a fair chance!

It didn't help that one of the next things he did was to say, "Even better than your pictures!" with a smirk and a tone that was all player.

I once heard that it takes five to ten seconds to form a first impression of someone and around thirty seconds to form a judgment. My first impression of Rob was enough for me to very quickly conclude that I had no interest in a second date with him.

I honestly do not recall details about the date, but I know that I gave it a genuine effort (and it was an effort). I don't even remember how it ended, but only about three days later, Rob texted me to see if I wanted to meet him at a park for some exercise. I genuinely could not make it due to a job interview, so out of guilt, I arranged another lunch date the following Monday, March 27th, at Rusty Bucket. That's where the story really begins.

It wasn't long into our conversation when Rob asked me why it had been so long since I had been in a serious relationship. He is a very curious guy and asks thought-provoking questions.

"You really want to know?" I asked.

"Yes!" he replied.

And from there, I testified to my love for Jesus and my desire to honor the Lord by remaining pure until I marry the one He sends. I spoke of how hard it is to find someone who shares the same love and desire for the Lord and that most men aren't interested in waiting until marriage.

And then it hit me that this was a Divine appointment. I watched as the Holy Spirit worked on Rob's heart with each word I spoke. Tears flowed from his eyes as he fought to hold them back but could not. Rob opened up and began confessing sins and strongholds that had taken hold of his life over the past year. Before we knew it, three hours had passed, and God had sown tremendous seeds into Rob's soul. He was clearly after Rob's heart, and apparently, He knew that I would be able to get his attention.

I did not realize that same day was also Rob's birthday. As we walked out to the car, he looked down at me and said that I was an angel, "a birthday gift sent from God." He then asked if he could give me a hug. I was never more thrilled to have had lunch with someone than that day. I no longer wanted to avoid Rob; on the contrary, I could not wait to talk with him again.

The next couple of weeks were filled with endless hours talking with Rob about the Lord. Other than a weekend when Rob was moving, we were pretty much inseparable. Of course, I was still unemployed, so I had a lot of free hours. My favorite thing in the world to do is evangelize to a seeking heart about Jesus, so my days were filled with energy as I poured into him and prayed for him daily. My insides raced with excitement!

Coupled with the joy of evangelizing, my heart was stirred with the hope that I had just met my husband. I had been waiting for years (decades, actually) for God's promise to be fulfilled in my life. Could Rob be the one I had been waiting for? I was doing everything in my power to take it slowly, but my heart raced ahead with hope as the days continued.

I knelt before the Lord one day and asked, "Lord, may I pursue this relationship?" I distinctly recall Him answering "yes." Whether I realized it or not, at that moment, I had concluded that I had found my husband. But at this subtle moment, I began to lose connection with the Lord.

I was incredibly conflicted within. On one hand, Rob was the first guy in many years that I could envision starting a relationship with. He checked many of the boxes I had in mind for what I wanted. On the other hand, I was concerned about how spiritually inexperienced he was. But the Lord told me He was my husband, right? I had to trust in the Lord's guidance.

In just a few weeks, Rob and I agreed to date one another exclusively.

The beginning held many bumps and bruises. As I stated earlier, purity was my utmost priority, which meant there would be no sexual activity of any kind prior to marriage. That was hard for Rob. He was young in his faith and had not yet reached that conviction. To him, if you truly loved someone, then sex was simply a reflection of that love. For me to deny him in this way only left him feeling less of a man.

In addition, our times together were intensely filled with spiritual content. On the one hand, he was hungry and sprinting to learn all he could; on the other hand, it was like drinking from a fire hose and often left him feeling inadequate. At one point, he even suggested we break up because it was all just too much for him. Somewhere deep in my spirit, I actually believed that breaking up would be best for us, but nothing in my flesh was willing to accept that because I desperately wanted him to be the one God had chosen. And I was convinced God had told me he was the one. *So I ignored the still, small voice.*

Nonetheless, Rob and I worked through every bump along the way and always seemed to come out united. The only place there was division was in my heart and spirit; there was a war going on inside of me. Something was "off," but I let my mind get in the way of what was happening in my spirit.

There were even signs to indicate that God was calling us to slow down. For example, Rob and I spent a few days at a cabin in Indiana, one of my favorite things to do. I planned the whole trip, including a surprise time on some four-wheelers in the woods. Oddly, one early evening as we sat by a campfire, a turtle crossed our path alongside the gravel drive.

That's strange, I thought. A turtle crossing the gravel drive-way way out in the middle of nowhere (the cabin was even named The Middle of Nowhere!). There were a couple of other times that weekend when turtles also showed up. Had I been paying attention, I would have realized the Holy Spirit was speaking to us through symbolism: a turtle represents a slow pace, and the Lord was trying to tell us to take things slowly. Slowly doesn't mean stopping the pursuit of the relationship, right? So, I continued the dance, assuming we just needed to make sure we slowed down the process. This made sense to me, given that I had been down similar roads before.

However, Jeremiah reminds us, "The heart is deceitful above all things, and desperately wicked, who can know it?" (17:9, KJV). Rob was baptized, which was great, but the months following the baptism were marked with struggles in our relationship. I continued to grow weary from the conflict within, and Rob and I struggled more and more with the physical longings that naturally accompany a dating relationship.

Is it really supposed to be this hard? I would ask myself.

Then the Lord began to speak louder regarding His intentions for our relationship. On one occasion, He used a dear friend of mine to ask me a series of poignant questions about whether Rob was the one. Every question cut right to the heart, confirming what I already knew all along. I started to see that I had misunderstood the Lord's intention for this relationship. I had been dancing a different dance than the Lord had planned. Yet I was not ready to face my new reality.

On another occasion, one of my closest girlfriends called me with what she believed was a message from the Lord. The reality is that she was spot on in what the Lord had spoken to her.

"What I am about to say is incredibly hard for me. I don't like confrontation," she said. "But I believe the Lord has already told you that Rob is not the one."

Every word she spoke cut me like a double-edged sword. The Lord *had* already spoken to my spirit, which confirmed the truth yet again. There was no avoiding it; God was turning up the heat and sounding the trumpet.

Doubts flooded my mind; fear flooded my soul. Looking back, I can clearly see that my flesh was waging war against the spirit.

> **"THE CARNAL MIND IS ENMITY AGAINST GOD: FOR IT IS NOT SUBJECT TO THE LAW OF GOD, NEITHER INDEED CAN BE."**
> —ROMANS 8:7, KJV

Oh, how hard my flesh fought to find a loophole or to justify why the words she spoke may not be true. God asked me to place that one most valued treasure (marriage) on the altar with no sure sign that it would be returned. It felt as though my insides were being ripped apart and something inside me was dying. And it was. The pain of walking against the leading of the Holy Spirit far outweighed the pain of losing the greatest desire of my heart. I could no longer continue the disconnect I had with Jesus. Eventually, I ended my relationship with Rob.

At that moment, I was filled with a peace I had not felt in ten months. My connection with the Lord was restored.

As the weeks and months went by, I learned things about Rob's life that confirmed it best that we break up for his sake and mine. I was incredibly grateful that I chose to heed God's voice. Had I ignored the Lord's guidance and remained on the path I was on, these hidden things may have resulted in painful consequences for us both. God knows best, and He truly desires to protect His children.

* * *

Recovery was a process more than it was an event. I had to come to terms with the fact that I would mourn the loss of something I cared deeply about, something I had invested much of my soul into. I could not flip a switch and turn off the pain. I also had to forgive myself for misunderstanding what God meant when He said I could pursue a relationship with Rob—the very place I lost connection with Him.

God was so gracious through it all. Being the faithful Father He is, He showed up to minister to me in my despondency. I distinctly remember Him addressing the unspoken thoughts in my mind. At one point, as I lay on my bed, I began to see a vision of a bush slowly growing, and as I inquired of the Lord, He impressed upon my heart that healing takes time and that I would eventually be pleased with the results. I sensed that one day Rob and I would be healed enough to be in each other's presence without going back. The Lord met me at every corner to lead me in a dance of freedom from my despair.

This too, is grace.

> **"THERE HATH NO TEMPTATION TAKEN YOU BUT SUCH AS IS COMMON TO MAN: BUT GOD IS FAITHFUL, WHO WILL NOT SUFFER YOU TO BE TEMPTED ABOVE THAT YE ARE ABLE; BUT WILL WITH THE TEMPTATION ALSO MAKE A WAY TO ESCAPE, THAT YE MAY BE ABLE TO BEAR IT."**
> —1 CORINTHIANS 10:13, KJV

8

RESPONDING IN REPENTANCE

The Cost of True Freedom

While grace is an unmerited gift and offers amazing power, it is by no means a license to live in sin. Repentance has always been a part of the equation for believers, whether regarding the mercy of the Old Testament or the grace of the New.

To repent means to change your mind about something, which leads to a change of action that aligns with what God desires.

THE PRIDE OF PERFECTIONISM

Perfectionists set such unrealistically high standards, standards of flawlessness that only Jesus could attain but that they believe they can, and *should*, attain for themselves. Pastor Dave Dunham expands on this.

> Failure to attain this level is unacceptable, in their mind. Not attaining that level of perfection then becomes a source of sorrow, frustration, and discouragement in the life of a perfectionist. They become irritable, annoyed,

and angry. They can tend to make excuses, blame others, or beat themselves up for failure. Some become consumed with working harder next time, achieving that unattainable goal. Others decide not to even try anymore, but simply to quit before they get started so that they don't have to face the failure.[14]

If this level of flawlessness were achievable or expected, none of us would have needed a Savior to intercede and fill in the gap where we lacked. But pride refuses to surrender to the reality that the standard was met through Jesus and cannot be achieved by man's efforts.

Proverbs 16:5 says, "The Lord detests all the proud of heart" (NIV). Rick Thomas explains why this is.

"The bottom line is that the wannabe perfectionist is unwilling to totally trust God. The great sadness is the commentary they are making about the Gospel. That is, they are saying that God's acceptance through the finished work of His Son is not good enough. They need a little more approval— Jesus plus others equals everything."[15]

To align with God and His ways, we must repent of our perfectionism.

* * *

The other side of this coin deserves mention: not everyone enters into perfectionism intending to be arrogant or puffed up, the very definition of pride. I shared earlier that my perfectionism was birthed out of fear and rejection, ultimately leading to shame (the belief that I am worthless). Repenting from perfectionism can mean the need to repent from the lies associated with shame.

Shame says that I am a mistake. God says that He created me on purpose. (See Psalm 139:14.)

Shame says I am bad and, therefore, can never be worth anything. God says that there is no one who is good, yet He died for all. (See Psalm 14:3, Romans 3:10, and Romans 5:8.)

Shame says man's opinion defines my worth. God says His opinion of me trumps all others. (See Psalm 118:5–9.)

Shame says I am unlovable. God says He died for me even when I was living in my transgressions and that I am more valuable than many sparrows. (See Ephesians 2:1 and Matthew 10:31.) He loves me regardless of my status.

To continue to live in shame means one must believe his or her worth is defined by someone or something else other than the Lord. As I have already established, this is not the gospel.

This is where the grace and compassion of God come in; He understands the *reasons* behind perfectionism and is merciful in the process of leading you to repentance. His patience, combined with His willingness to reveal His grace, has given you everything you need to repent. As it says in Proverbs, "By *mercy and truth iniquity is purged:* and by the fear of the Lord men depart from evil." (16:6, KJV)

In the Christian realm, it is common to refer to repentance as turning away from sin. Emphasis is typically placed on the behaviors you need to start or stop doing, yet very little, if any, emphasis is placed on the role of the Holy Spirit in the process. This can be detrimental to a perfectionist.

Again, the first several years of my walk with the Lord were full of zeal and passion for God's word; I couldn't get enough of it. My perfectionist self loved the rules that Scripture provided such as:

"All wrongdoing is sin."
—1 John 5:17, NIV

"[W]hoever knows the right thing to do and
fails to do it, for him it is sin."
—James 4:17, ESV

"The acts of the sinful nature are obvious: sexual immo-
rality, impurity and debauchery; idolatry and witchcraft;
hatred, discord, jealousy, fits of rage, selfish ambition,
dissensions, factions, and envy; drunkenness, orgies, and
the like. I warn you, as I did before, that those who live
like this will not inherit the kingdom of God."
—Galatians 5:19–21, NIV

The level of discipline I applied to my natural health
translated nicely into my spiritual health. I quickly developed
spiritual muscle in my efforts to live a sinless life. If a temptation came my way, I could resist it. If I already had sin in
my life, I stopped it. At first, I did extraordinarily well, but
there came the point when I faced a sin that I could not stop
doing, no matter how hard I tried. Oh, I would have victory
for a time (I actually went seven years once!), but then failure
inevitably ensued. That's when I realized there's more to this
process than I understood.

Here's what I missed: any victory I had obtained to that
point happened *through my own strength*. Let me explain.

Repentance always begins with a choice. I had to *decide* to
deny the temptation that was before me—which is actually
the right place to start. The error was leaning on my own
strength to get through it; I often white-knuckled my way to
victory. You know, that place where you hold on to something
so hard and tight to endure it as if your life depended on it.
Yet all the while, my insides were exhausted and tied up in a
ball of stress. On a subconscious level, I was driven by fear of
punishment, terribly worried that if I sinned, I would be in
big trouble with the Lord. The approach may have resulted in

obedience, but it lacked one major component: *the grace of God*. God does not desire repentance motivated by fear, which is tormenting, but rather from a result of discovering His love.

> **"THERE IS NO FEAR IN LOVE; BUT PERFECT LOVE CASTETH OUT FEAR: BECAUSE FEAR HATH TORMENT. HE THAT FEARETH IS NOT MADE PERFECT IN LOVE."**
>
> —1 JOHN 4:18, KJV

Without realizing it at the time, I had fallen from grace and was operating in a place where I believed I must overcome sin by my own strength *to be acceptable to God*. This faulty belief led to an approach that ultimately was not sustainable. While I may, at times, have avoided the act of sinning, I never truly overcame it, and I lacked major peace within. Ultimately, I was disconnected from my relationship with the Lord.

* * *

Has there ever been a time in your life when there was something in your way that was a major obstacle, and you wanted it moved, but it was too heavy to move it yourself, so you had to call someone to help, and when he or she came to your side, the two of you removed the barrier together? You relied on their strength to help you through even though there was still work to do on your part.

The process of repentance is similar, except now you are engaging with the Creator of the universe, who holds far more power than a natural friend. In those moments of need, He invites you to ask Him to help you remove the obstacle. In return, He delights in providing His grace to help you confront the temptation. Notice what the Scripture tells us:

"Let us therefore come boldly unto the throne of grace,
that we may obtain mercy, and *find grace
to help in time of need."*
—Hebrews 4:16, KJV

"And he said unto me, "My grace is sufficient for thee:
for *my strength is made perfect in [your] weakness."*
—2 Corinthians 12:9, KJV

"For we do not have a High Priest who cannot sympa-
thize with our weaknesses, but *was in all points
tempted as we are*, yet without sin."
—Hebrews 4:15, NKJV

With the grace of God comes the love and understanding that knows you cannot succeed in your walk without His help. Furthermore, "The Lord is *merciful and gracious, slow to anger*, and plenteous in mercy." (Psalm 103:8, KJV) He never intended for you to perfect yourself; He will perfect you. Your job is to work *with Him* in the process, leaning on His power.

> **"BUT THE GOD OF ALL GRACE, WHO HATH CALLED US UNTO HIS ETERNAL GLORY BY CHRIST JESUS, AFTER THAT YE HAVE SUFFERED A WHILE, MAKE YOU PERFECT, STABLISH, STRENGTHEN, SETTLE YOU."**
>
> —1 PETER 5:10, KJV

DELIVERANCE

Many Christians never truly overcome sin because they do not understand the Lord's role in the process. They walk around forgiven but can't understand why they habitually struggle with the same sin. Their soul is like a leaky cistern that can't hold the Spirit's power within, and every time they repeat the unhealthy behavior, a little more of that power drains from them until their walk with the Lord has little-to-no impact on the world around them. Through my struggles, I can look upon others with compassion as they wrestle through their process of overcoming.

On the flip side, when a Christian struggles with a particular temptation or habitual sin, recognizes it and humbly turns to God for the power (grace) to resist it, the result is victory. Repeated victory results in overcoming the thing that once held that person in bondage; in other words, when the temptation comes, that person has exercised repentance enough that he or she has developed the strength to no longer give in to the temptation like before. Repentance yields grace; grace yields a true and *sustainable* victory.

If you have ever heard someone use the phrase, "I have been *delivered* from lust/alcoholism/drug addiction/gossip/ etc." they are referencing this kind of overcoming. They are no longer in bondage to the power the sin had over them but instead can deny it on a regular and consistent basis by leaning on the grace of God. Additionally, that person usually has certain compassion and patience toward others who are struggling, combined with power birthed from having wrestled through the process themselves. An overcomer becomes someone who can make a positive impact on other lives by helping others do the same.

> **"I CAN DO ALL THINGS THROUGH CHRIST WHO STRENGTHENS ME."**
> —PHILIPPIANS 4:13, NKJV

9

MAINTAINING YOUR GARDEN

Making Room for Grace in the Garden of Your Soul

Have you ever been in a situation where your boss gave out a special assignment to the team, and by the time each team member returned with their results, everyone had accomplished the goal differently? In other words, there's more than one way to skin a cat. I believe the path to accessing grace is no different. God gives us an abundance of tools that are essential to cultivating fertile soil in our soul, free from the host of lies that grow like weeds and choke out the peace that is our God-given right. How and when you use those tools may vary along the journey, though they are necessary, nonetheless. With time and consistency, you will be amazed at what is possible.

PRAYER

At the most basic level, prayer simply means talking with God. Key to prayer is *intentional and active* communication with Him versus passive meditation.

If you think about it, talking with God is very similar to talking with a friend or relative. At times it may mean a one-sided conversation where you are doing all the talking. At other times, someone else may need you to be a listening ear. And finally, you both may engage in back-and-forth dialogue. The type of conversations can vary from sharing excitement to problem-solving, venting, asking various questions, and even sharing heartbreak.

My conversations with God are really no different.

Most often, when I need God's grace, my conversations with Him range somewhere between requesting His help and begging for it. The hard part is learning to tell when there is still a disconnect between your head and your heart, and you approach Him for His grace but still try to operate in your own strength. This is very normal while this spiritual muscle gets exercised, but eventually, you will learn to tell the difference.

> "FOR WE DO NOT HAVE A HIGH PRIEST WHO IS UNABLE TO EMPATHIZE WITH OUR WEAKNESSES, BUT WE HAVE ONE WHO HAS BEEN TEMPTED IN EVERY WAY, JUST AS WE ARE—YET HE DID NOT SIN. LET US THEN APPROACH GOD'S THRONE OF GRACE WITH CONFIDENCE, SO THAT WE MAY RECEIVE MERCY AND FIND GRACE TO HELP US IN OUR TIME OF NEED."
>
> —HEBREWS 4:15, 16, NIV

Our Heavenly Father is just waiting for you to humbly ask Him for help! I once heard someone describe Him as a gentleman: He never forces us, but if we are willing to come to Him, He loves to provide mercy and grace when we need it. Every step toward Him in this type of communion is like having your own personal gardener who can help you identify and uproot the weeds of lies that have grown in your belief system—what a glorious gift we have been given.

* * *

I still journal. Since the time my Christian journey began in my mid-twenties, I have written close to thirty journals! At some point, journaling became another form of prayer for me. Oftentimes, I have found that I can better communicate my thoughts by writing; other times, I find it easier to sort things out. Some of my most authentic conversations with God happened while writing to Him.

Maybe it's because I prefer to process externally, or maybe it has to do with the fact that writing and speaking use two different brain systems, so something happens differently with one than the other.[16] Either way, there are times when journaling empowers me to tap into God's grace like nothing else.

PRAISE

According to scholars, there are several types of praise. The word can mean many things to many people and usually connotes thanksgiving and blessing. More often than not, in my experience, praise is used interchangeably with worship, though if you dig deeper into the root meanings of each, you might realize some key differences between them. Nonetheless, at its core, praise is another weapon that can lead you to victory.

In 2 Chronicles 20, you see the children of Ammon and Moab come against Jehoshaphat to battle, along with a great multitude. After learning of the magnitude of the threat, Jehoshaphat grows fearful and immediately calls a fast throughout all of Judah and turns to the Lord to ask for help, reminding Him of who He is and what He has promised. From there, the Spirit of God comes upon Jahaziel, the son of Zechariah, in the midst of the congregation, causing him to encourage them all that God would be with them and not fear because the battle would be His.

71

The following day as they prepared to march forth, Jehoshaphat encouraged everyone to believe in the prophecy given through Jahaziel so that they would prosper. Notice what happened from there:

> [W]hen he [Jehoshaphat] had consulted with the people, he appointed singers unto the Lord, and that should praise the beauty of holiness, as they went out before the army, and to say, Praise the Lord; for his mercy endureth forever. And when they began to sing and to praise, the Lord set ambushments against the children of Ammon, Moab, and mount Seir, which were come against Judah; and they were smitten.
>
> —2 Chronicles 20:21–22, KJV

As a perfectionist, I picture my enemy being the religious spirit that often seems too big for me to conquer. I find myself time and again falling out of grace as I have for so many years, and then I remember this beautiful example of the steps I can take to step back into flow with God:

I can remember His role as my Defender, who fights the battle for me.

I can turn to Him in prayer and ask for help.

I can praise Him from a posture of belief that He will do what He promises to do.

I can watch my enemy be smitten.

I believe one of the key things that happens when we praise God is that we have a change of focus. Instead of having our eyes on ourselves and our circumstances, we look away to God, and all of a sudden, our mind is in perfect peace, just like it says will happen in Isaiah 26:3 (KJV): "Thou wilt keep him in perfect peace, whose mind is stayed on thee: because he trusteth in thee."

If we are focused on Him and are at peace within, we will also avoid complaining, negativity, and all of the other bad fruit that results from focusing on ourselves.

Another key thing that praising God does is usher in God's presence.

The way I see it, if God is present, the enemy is not!

> **"BUT THOU ART HOLY, O THOU THAT INHABITEST THE PRAISES OF ISRAEL."**
> —PSALM 22:3, KJV

* * *

For me, praise takes many forms. Sometimes I verbally bless Him for all He has done for us and who He is. Other times, praise takes the form of playing music and singing to Him with my hands raised in the air as if to give Him all of me. I praise Him in my journal writings with a posture of gratitude, thanking Him for all things I can think of at that moment. I even have times when praise is a sacrifice, as Scripture says, that needs to happen despite how I feel, simply because He deserves it. How you choose to praise is completely up to you.

Ultimately, praise shifts your focus back to the One who holds power. It changes your internal abiding place from the natural realm to the spiritual one. When you abide in Jesus and dwell on His perspectives, your internal atmosphere will change. You will begin to be filled with hope, peace, and many other life-giving fruits. It is as if praising is a mega-fertilizer that enhances all the good fruit that blooms within you.

When you live a life of praise, you can conquer just about anything!

MULTIPLE COUNSELORS

I have found this biblical principle incredibly helpful through the years as I battled perfectionism. I know that this may come easier for extroverts and external processors, but there is a reason God declared this as a kingdom principle. When you seek counsel from others, you allow God's Spirit to work through them and benefit each of you.

> **"WHERE NO COUNSEL IS, THE PEOPLE FALL: BUT IN THE MULTITUDE OF COUNSELORS THERE IS SAFETY."**
>
> —PROVERBS 11:14, KJV

I recommend that you seek those who are trustworthy, who will be honest with you no matter what, and who are Spirit-led. It is critical that your counselors can discern if a religious spirit is present, and if you are trapped in a snare and fallen from grace.

My greatest struggle was believing that God wanted me to accept grace, for I had lived for so long under the pressure and condemnation of the religious spirit. If I were to describe my typical interactions with God each day, it consisted of me approaching Him with striving in my heart, begging Him to help me do better, be better, repent, change, and any other performance-like posture you can think of. I always had a list of things that I believed needed to change about me so that I would be a better Christian. Without realizing it, I started every single day from a place of needing to perform to be accepted.

When I first began realizing there was a problem and that I was in some kind of bondage, I reached out to some Christian sisters in the faith who were experienced in something called inner healing, which is a Spirit-led approach to healing. I immediately scheduled a visit and drove several hundred miles from Ohio to Illinois to meet with them. That was the beginning of the revelation of the religious spirit's stronghold over me (though I hadn't connected it with perfectionism at that point).

The next several years involved more of these sessions and many phone calls as I navigated the confusion. As God showed up, He began emphasizing His mercy, compassion, kindness, and long-suffering, yet I had the hardest time believing it was really Him. I actually thought it was a counterfeit, and I was being deceived. As I stated, I had been used to that voice that chimed in my ear consistently, telling me I was not doing enough, was not good enough, and needed to change everything to be welcomed and loved.

Every trusted spiritual counselor I sought help from bore witness to the fact that God was leading me to His grace and that I was being set free from a religious spirit.

Eventually, God began to show up and speak things to me directly that indicated His desire for me to be kinder to myself, rest more, cease striving, and myriad other messages flowing from His grace. Sometimes as I prayed, I would immediately get words like "couch" or "pillow" that intersected in my Spirit while I was striving in prayer with God. The more it happened, the more I realized that it might be Him, so I would pause and press into prayer until I realized He was using those words to indicate His desire for me to simply rest—spiritual promptings don't always have to be mysterious!

At other times, when the religious spirit had me believing I wasn't perfect enough physically and I would be tearing myself down with critical self-talk, God would show up in a similar manner and say things like, "You are beautiful," or "Your hair looks great curly." Again, it happened enough times at first that I had to pay attention to it, pray about it, and listen to what God was saying. And as I shared with others in my life, they confirmed that God was truly helping me see truth through His eyes. As you share, others will either agree or not, and you will begin to see a pattern that helps you realize what is true.

> **"IN THE MOUTH OF TWO OR THREE WITNESSES SHALL EVERY WORD BE ESTABLISHED."**
> —2 CORINTHIANS 13:1, KJV

It has taken years for me to accept these truths! Like Paul, I have had to be persuaded that it aligned with God's perspective. (See 2 Timothy 1:12, KJV) The process could not have happened without help from others. I firmly believe I could not have gotten this far without them. If I can encourage you with anything, it would be this: We are not meant to walk this thing alone. Trust God's principles, seek help, and find your safety in a multitude.

INVENTORY THE FRUIT

If I asked you what kind of fruit tree was in my backyard, you would look out the back window to see what kind of fruit the tree produces. The fruit helps us understand what kind of tree it is.

Our thoughts and emotions are similar.

Have you ever stopped to inventory your thoughts and emotions, especially on a day when you find yourself depressed, anxious, oppressed, or confused? These emotions are examples of bad fruit that have to be coming from something other than Jesus, who is our Tree of Life. When Jesus is the source, Scripture says, "The fruit of the Spirit is love, joy, peace, patience, kindness, goodness, faithfulness, gentleness, and self-control" (Galatians 5:22–23, ESV).

Anything else is not rooted in Him.

Throughout my journey to discovering grace, I have learned to discern when my fruit is bad and rooted in the lies of the enemy versus in Jesus's ways. For example, every morning when I started my day, I had in mind a list of what I needed to get done that day. Trust me when I say that my to-do list typically exceeded what most people would consider a normal amount of production for one day; nonetheless, as far as I was concerned, my expectation was all that mattered.

I fully accept that life throws curve balls that will disrupt our plans and prevent us from completing our tasks. However, if I began to slack off for no apparent reason, or somehow I just didn't feel like completing the entire list, I would begin to mentally enter into self-condemnation, which undoubtedly led to oppression and depression (bad fruit). To leave a task undone when I expected myself to get it done was unacceptable. Little did I realize that I was living in perfectionism, much less that perfectionism was a bad fruit.

You will do well to consider looking for similar patterns in your own life. Take note of what you are thinking and feeling each day. Do you have internal peace? Are you at rest and living in the moment or striving and feeling pressure to get things done a certain way or time? Are you exhausted? These can all be indicators of bad fruit that you can safely conclude are coming from a source other than Jesus.

> "**BE NOT CONFORMED TO THIS WORLD: BUT BE YE TRANSFORMED BY THE RENEWING OF YOUR MIND, THAT YE MAY PROVE WHAT IS THAT GOOD, AND ACCEPTABLE, AND PERFECT, WILL OF GOD.**"
> —ROMANS 12:2, KJV

RENEWING THE MIND

I have good news! There is a way out from the frequent bad fruit you may be experiencing.

The original Greek word for renewing is *anakainōsis*, which refers to a renovation or a complete change for the better.[17]

Technically speaking, when you put your faith in Jesus and decide to follow Him, Scripture says you are "given the mind of Christ" (1 Corinthians 2:16, KJV) and become a "new creature" (2 Corinthians 5:17, KJV). In essence, because His Spirit now lives inside your spirit, you have direct access to Him and His nature. By His grace, you are given all of the riches in Christ, which includes knowledge of His truth and His ways.

One of my favorite scenes from *The Matrix* is when the main character, Neo, is hooked up to a computer system that downloads Kung Fu directly to his brain. Neo awakes and simply says, "I know Kung Fu," and when the situation called for it, Neo was able to take action immediately.

I would love to tell you that we could approach our walk with Jesus in the same way; however, though we now have direct access to His mind and have been made a new creature, it does not mean we automatically think like He thinks or do what He does. When the marriage happened between the Holy Spirit and you, two natures became one—His nature inside your imperfect human vessel. That means that there is an ongoing process where we have to "put off the old self with its former lusts," as it says in Ephesians 4, and "put on the new man and be renewed in the spirit of your mind" (22–24, KJV).

* * *

The mind is the command center of the body. It sends signals that control thought, memory, emotion, touch, motor skills, vision, breathing, temperature, hunger and every process that regulates our body. Over time, as these signals get repeated, it creates a neural network of pathways that lead to habitual responses, similar to a computer's operating system that functions only in certain ways or the grooves on a vinyl record that play the same song over and over.

To renew the mind, you have to give it a new operating system—or play a new song, if you will. The old adage, "You reap what you sow," could not be more accurate. Whatever we feed our brain with, whatever we think about, everything else will follow. It all starts in the mind.

Practically speaking, this is where you come in.

As I began to have truth revealed to me by the Holy Spirit, I began rehearsing those truths on a daily basis. Belief systems have muscle memory; rewiring them requires work, and they don't go down without a fight. Remember, this is also a spiritual battle, and the principalities of the air do not like to see God's children being set free. They know God's Word and who wins the battle. If they can keep you out of intimacy with your Heavenly Father, they can eliminate the power of His Kingdom over darkness.

"Have you been in the Word today, Leneé?" the voices whisper.

"You're still struggling with that sin? God will never accept you if you keep doing that. How can you call yourself a Christian?" the old song sings.

"Did you see how your neck is starting to sag now that you are entering a new decade? You are starting to look old," says the inner critic.

"You don't have that done yet? Hurry up, Pezzano. You are never going to get anywhere in life," says the hidden taskmaster.

Does any of this sound familiar? Yet hear what Paul has to say about the people of God:

"We are destroying arguments and all arrogance raised against the knowledge of God, and we are taking every thought captive to the obedience of Christ."

—2 Corinthians 10:5, NASB

We have to be intentional and proactive about it. When the thoughts come, we must capture them and reroute them. And if the thoughts haven't come yet, we must anticipate they will and proactively ward them off.

Write the truth down on post-it notes where you can see it frequently, say it out loud as your drive, or cover your journal pages with it. Every time you rehearse God's truths to yourself, you are playing your brain a new song, and your faith grows. Let your ear hear until your brain starts recognizing the new patterns. *Your brain will do what you tell it to do.* Here are some truths to get you started:

I am a child of the King.

I do not have to earn God's love; I am accepted into His Kingdom because of my faith in the Blood of Jesus.

I am not expected to be perfect, but only to follow Him with my whole heart.

By His Spirit, the consequence of my sin nature has been paid for. His love now covers my sins, and He will equip me to grow in Him.

Romans 10:17 tells us that "faith comes from *hearing*, and hearing by the Word of God." (NKJV) Keep declaring the truth; everything else will follow.

GRACE TO SELF

This is the one area I struggle with the most. It is very natural for me to default to negative self-talk or compare myself to others through a lens of believing they are better than I in every way. Not only do I treat myself poorly on a regular basis, but I very rarely *want* to be intentional about rewiring my perspective to align with God's. And you and I both know that when you don't want to do something, it is very difficult to make yourself do it. It comes down to the power of choice and deciding to show myself grace.

The problem is that when I choose to walk according to our flesh and not the Spirit, I am not repenting and allowing the Lord to deliver me from the root issue of perfectionism. As long as I feed the beast, it will grow, and I will never walk in true freedom. Remember, when you change your thinking, everything else will follow. In essence, you must pull the weeds of wrong beliefs, plant new seeds of truth, and cultivate them regularly until the garden of your soul is filled with good fruit.

> **"FOR AS [A MAN] THINKETH IN HIS HEART, SO IS HE."**
> —PROVERBS 23:7, KJV

So I must choose life and do so repeatedly until it sticks.

I began to see real progress when I gave myself permission to make mistakes. Regardless of the size of the mistake, I *quickly* took my thoughts captive and channeled them toward self-forgiveness. The less time I spent beating myself up, the better. My self-talk looked something like this:

"It's okay. You are not alone. Everyone messes up."

"You didn't intentionally set out to do this."

"You were never going to be able to do everything perfectly, which is why you have Jesus. Forgive yourself and know that you will make plenty more mistakes."

Additionally, I have learned to give myself a pep talk *before* I ever start a task, especially one that feels hard and that I really want to procrastinate. The more I can set my expectations that mistakes are likely, the more I can embrace them when they come.

Over time, my heart has caught up to my head; in other words, I actually believe in my heart that it is okay to make mistakes versus just knowing it in my head. Today, it's now more natural to forgive myself for a mistake than it is to beat myself up. This is a true transformation that started with showing grace to myself.

One of the best recommendations I have heard when it comes to showing grace to yourself is to consider talking to yourself the way you would talk to your closest friend. More often than not, you would never repeatedly tell your friend how much they suck at something or don't deserve forgiveness to the point of shaming them. Neither should you do the same to yourself.

If you can put this principle into practice, you will be amazed at how God's grace transforms your life. You will begin to experience freedom as you have never known. Your mind will feel lighter as you no longer carry an overdeveloped sense of responsibility, you will begin to see the world differently, and joy will replace a burdened heart. Others will see the difference, and before you know it, your relationships will grow richer and stronger. Importantly, your ability to connect with God will be unstoppable. Not only can His grace get you there, but it will keep you there. And in every situation, His power can work through you because of your willingness to accept your weaknesses. Notice what Paul says in Scripture:

"And he said unto me, My grace is sufficient for thee: for *my strength is made perfect in weakness*. Most gladly therefore will I rather glory in my infirmities, that the power of Christ may rest upon me."

—2 Corinthians 12:9, KJV

Paul did not live by misguided expectations; he clearly knew that only by the grace of God could he accomplish anything of value in life and truly live out his destiny on earth. My prayer is for you to understand the same.

PART 4

THE RENEWAL

10

A MERCIFUL ASSURANCE

God's Redemptive Love

As I have insisted throughout this book, the entire Christian journey is about *relationship*—with oneself, others, and with the Heavenly Father. From the beginning of creation, relationship with man was at the center of all He said and did; it was His very heart. No other living thing was held in as high esteem as humans. After our disobedience destroyed our relationship with the Heavenly Father, He came to us and died for us so that our relationship with Him could be restored. God chose man above every other created being. His heart has always been, and will always be, for you.

The word *relationship* is not easily found in Scripture, nor is it found in every version. The few times I have found it, it refers to things connected through circumstances, like business dealings, but not the kind of connection describing intimacy between two people who share a deep emotional or spiritual connection beyond the intellect into the heart. The exception is in John 1:18, which says, "No one has ever seen God, but the one and only Son, who is himself God and is *in closest relationship* with the Father, has made him known" (NIV).

In the original language, "in closest relationship" refers to the situation where Jesus has His head lying on the bosom of the Father. One does not lay his or her head on someone's bosom unless there is a connection that goes well beyond a business relationship.

Have you ever laid your head on the bosom of someone you are close with? What did you hear? If you lie there long enough, you begin to hear the beating of his or her heart. I don't believe it is a coincidence that our hearts are physically located where our bosoms are. God knew all along that the natural would be a metaphor for the spiritual; in other words, the way to know a person's heart would require a closeness in the relationship or a level of intimacy that goes much deeper than just an acquaintance or colleague.

How close did Jesus have to be to the Heavenly Father for him to say,

> For I have not spoken of myself; *but the Father* which sent me, he *gave me a commandment,* what I should say, and what I should speak. And I know that his commandment is life everlasting: whatsoever I speak therefore, even as the Father said unto me, so I speak.
>
> —John 12:49, KJV

All that Jesus did flowed *from* His relationship with the Father, not *to* earn His acceptance.

You may be saying to yourself, "It's great that Jesus had such intimacy with the Father, but it's Jesus we are talking about; He was perfect."

He may have been perfect, but there was one who was far from it, maybe even worse than you or I. His name was King David.

David didn't start out being known for his mistakes. He was the youngest of eight sons and grew up in a family that bred sheep. He had chores much like you or I had growing up, though his consisted mainly of tending the flock. I would also imagine in a family that large, especially with all boys, there were times of sibling rivalry. All in all, David's beginnings weren't vastly different from yours or mine.

In that part of the world, tending sheep brought inherent dangers, such as the threat of dangerous wildlife. Whereas you or I would likely not encounter a bear or lion outside of the zoo, David dealt with the possibility of facing them daily until eventually the possibility became a reality and he killed both to save his lambs. He had begun to write his warrior resume.

Following those events, David was faced with another battle, only this time with a giant human from the Philistines named Goliath, who was threatening King Saul and scaring his people. I want you to hear what David says to Saul regarding the situation:

> But David said to Saul, "Your servant used to keep his father's sheep, and when a lion or a bear came and took a lamb out of the flock, I went out after it and struck it, and delivered the lamb from its mouth; and when it arose against me, I caught it by its beard, and struck and killed it. *Your servant has killed both lion and bear; and this uncircumcised Philistine will be like one of them, seeing he has defied the armies of the living God.*"
>
> —1 Samuel 17:34–36, NKJV

I am not clear when or how David knew the living God, but obviously, he did based on what he said to Saul with confidence. This guy knew what it meant to lean on the strength of God to win his battles.

Scripture tells us that David was a man after God's own heart. (See 1 Samuel 13:14)

I don't know about you, but as a person who struggles with perfectionism, I'm looking at David's track record and have already felt the temptation to compare myself to David—and I'm not coming out looking so hot!

"Yeah, maybe he was human and not perfect, but he was seriously far greater than I could ever be!" The thoughts flood my mind so easily. I mean, the guy goes on to write the entire Book of Psalms, not to mention becoming a King of Israel and Judah.

But there's way more to his story.

You see, David made some serious mistakes along the way, most of them after he had become king of his people.

For instance, he disobeyed God's will by taking a census of the Israelites. Here's the story:

> *Satan stood up against Israel, and provoked David to number Israel.* And David said to Joab and to the rulers of the people, "Go, number Israel from Beersheba even to Dan; and bring the number of them to me, that I may know it." And Joab answered, "The Lord make his people an hundred times so many more as they be: but, my lord the king, are they not all my lord's servants? *Why then doth my lord require this thing? Why will he be a cause of trespass to Israel?"* Nevertheless the king's word prevailed against Joab. And God was displeased with this thing.
>
> —1 Chronicles 21:1–4, 7, KJV

During those times, one was only allowed to count or number what belonged to him. Furthermore, David was beginning to act like other kings who depended on armies and taxes rather than God.[18]

If a census were commanded of God, there still had to be a ransom given (by those whose lives were counted) to atone for the counting. (See Exodus 30:12) David knew this already, which is why his conscience got the best of him after he sinned: "David said unto God, *I have sinned greatly*, because I have done this thing. But now, I beseech thee, do away the iniquity of thy servant, for I have done very foolishly." (1 Chronicles 21:8, KJV)

From there, God gave David a choice to pick one of three consequences for his sin, two that would come from other people and one that would come directly from the Lord.

Here is where I get amazed.

David chose the one that would come directly from the Lord. He understood the mercy of God to such a degree that he would rather suffer at the Lord's hand than man's.

With my history of perfectionism, I am guessing I would have chosen the opposite!

David had hidden pride that God exposed, yet God did not destroy him. God knew what was needed to humble David and bring him to a place in his character, fitting his role as a king. This is key to understanding God's ways.

The entire experience was led by God. He already knew what was in David's heart, and He orchestrated the events in David's life to bring about a maturity in him that had not been there before. God had a plan and purpose for David and loved him enough to discipline him.

God desires to be our *Father*, not our Master. If the requirement to never sin were truly what God expected, David would have been destroyed immediately.

> "**MY SON, DESPISE NOT THOU THE CHASTENING OF THE LORD, NOR FAINT WHEN THOU ARE REBUKED OF HIM. FOR WHOM THE LORD LOVETH, HE CHASTENETH, AND SCOURGETH EVERY SON WHOM HE RECEIVETH.**"
>
> —HEBREWS 12:5-6, KJV

Yes, there were still consequences to his choice; however, God showed mercy even then. His ways are always *redemptive;* He desires to save you from erroneous ways so you can be all He designed you to be.

* * *

As a perfectionist, receiving God's mercy and forgiveness has been incredibly hard for me, as you have heard me say. But I don't know if I could ever come back from the next couple of sins that David committed!

You may know the story. David's people had just defeated the Ammonites and besieged Rabbah, though David stayed back in Jerusalem. One evening, he walked out onto the roof of his house and spotted his neighbor, Bathsheba, bathing. His heart filled with lust for her, and he immediately enquired about her, only to find out she was married to a man named Uriah. But that did not stop David. He sent for her, brought her to his room to have sex with her, and ended up getting her pregnant.

I have always heard this story referred to as an adulterous affair, but if you pause for a moment and consider the times they lived in, Bathsheba had no choice but to obey the king's command. To many, this was an abuse of power, an act of rape.

The story gets worse. Upon learning of Bathsheba's pregnancy, David covered it up by murdering her husband, Uriah, through a secret strategy placing Uriah in the center of the hottest battle to increase his chance of being killed. Upon his death, David took Bathsheba as his wife, and she bore him a son.

We're told, not surprisingly, that "the thing that David had done displeased the Lord." (2 Samuel 11:27, KJV) God sent Nathan the prophet to David, where he told David a parable that illuminated the sin David committed. As David heard the parable, he discerned that the punishment for the man in the parable should be death. Little did he know that the parable was describing him until Nathan told him so.

David once again immediately owned his sin, turned to the Lord, and accepted whatever consequence God brought. Though God did not spare the son conceived out of rape, He spared David's life and even restored his household with the birth of another son, Solomon.

Here was a man who once served others before he was put on the throne, but once there, he abused his power in many ways, and no one challenged him. Yet God loved him enough to discipline, teach, and restore him.

As I write this, I sit and ponder the gravity of the sins committed by David. If I walk in perfectionism, I immediately assume God would destroy David for his actions, which seem the epitome of unrighteousness. And yet, God's mercy prevailed, and David continued to be known as a man after God's own heart. How can it be so?

I believe the answer is two-fold. In the case of David, God knew David would be one who would "repent well." In other words, being the God who knows everything, He knew David's heart despite the flaws in his character, and He knew David would own his sin, repent, and turn to God even more. Secondly, God had made a covenant with David, which He intended to keep that promised that David's throne would remain forever throughout all generations (See 2 Sam 7:16). God is a faithful keeper of His promises.

* * *

The old me who walked ignorantly in perfectionism looked at these situations and reflexively concluded that David's sins were far greater than anything I could ever commit; it's not uncommon for perfectionists to be critical of others. However, if I pause long enough to ponder the truth, I am no

LENEÉ PEZZANO

different than David was. I have hidden sin in my heart that could easily lead me to graver levels of sin if left undealt with.

"GOD DOES NOT SHOW FAVORITISM."

—ROMANS 2:11, NIV

Yet this I can remain sure of: my Heavenly Father knows exactly how and when to expose those areas and lead me into repentance. I can look at David's life and realize that if God were willing and able to show grace to David, surely He would do the same for me.

May you and I receive that truth even more.

11

AN EMPOWERING REST

Living in a State of Grace

As I reflect on the years I have spent striving with perfectionism, one thing stands out. I could not rest physically, emotionally, or spiritually. Often, people would say to me, "Leneé, you are meant to be a human BE-ing, not a human DO-ing!" I would hear the wisdom in their counsel, but more often than not, I was unable to permit myself to apply that wisdom to my life.

Mid-day naps? Entire Saturdays where you stay in your pajamas all day and binge watch your favorite movies while eating popcorn and ice cream? Not usually. On occasion, I still had a hard time mentally. It took me at least two days on vacation to wind down and accept that I did not need to be producing anything, and even longer for my mental state to catch up to the physical rest. My insides were always in motion.

It makes sense, right? If every day I believed that I had to perform a certain way to be accepted, then I was naturally going to operate in go-mode. Unfortunately, this developed a natural ability to strive rather than be led by God's Spirit.

Not only did this way of life eventually catch up to me, resulting in exhaustion, depression, frustration, and a nervous breakdown, it put a major wedge between myself and Papa God.

Have you ever had someone in your life whom you just couldn't connect with, no matter how much you wanted to? You tried and tried to have a relationship, but every time you were with him or her, their mind was somewhere else, they were not really present, and you were unable to connect.

I believe it is very similar with God, except He is the one longing to connect with you. Has your perfectionism had you dwelling somewhere else emotionally and mentally, or so busy that you have been unable to hear His still, small voice or sense the presence of His Spirit?

In Scripture, the word *rest* has several meanings. Some refer to the physical state, such as taking a nap or a break after a long journey. This is the kind of rest we are familiar with when we need to allow our bodies to recover their energy and strength. Importantly, there's another kind of rest in Scripture that refers to a state of peace, relief from anxiety, or a less rigorous confinement.[19] This state of rest is what God desires most for His people, for in that place, the Holy Spirit has room to lead you where He wants to take you.

> **"FOR HE THAT IS ENTERED INTO HIS REST, HE ALSO HATH CEASED FROM HIS OWN WORKS, AS GOD DID FROM HIS."**
>
> —HEBREWS 4:10, KJV

This is where you cease working in your own strength and enter into the grace I have described throughout this book.

Not only does this state of rest give you the ability to connect with God and hear His voice more clearly, but it empowers you with the energy to produce!

"Wasn't this about doing less?" you might be asking.

Not necessarily. There are certainly many of us who could benefit from doing less. But what if you are the mom of several children who all require your attention on a daily basis, in addition to being the wife of someone who is a leader in your church, all while attempting to have your own relationship with God? Sometimes life does not allow you to do less in the natural realm. However, there is a place you can enter with the Lord where you cease from your own strength, wisdom, and expectations, and you lean on His grace that will empower you to complete all that is required of you. This is the empowering rest He longs for you to live.

There was a point in my career when I was named campus president for a small proprietary college in a suburb of Columbus, OH. A position with that level of authority also required a great deal of energy to meet the demands of students, staff, and the community daily. It took everything in me to keep the organization running.

One season, in particular, my family experienced some very challenging events involving my dad's health. His heart was failing, and we were unsure if he would live. For months we were back and forth to the hospital, feeling blessed that his defibrillator kept him alive more than once. On multiple occasions, I sat in hotel rooms and lobbies, juggling work and the many responsibilities of being a caretaker. To say it was wearying is an understatement. I realize as I look back that most of the time, I could not maintain rest in any form. Our family was in a storm. On rare occasions, I could connect with the Lord, lean on His strength, and meet the needs of my job as well as my father, all while maintaining a sense of peace and joy. This is empowering rest.

The perfectionist in me hates that I couldn't even struggle perfectly (it's a plague, isn't it?). Looking back, I see how much I lacked true rest because I didn't believe God would take care of me. Today, I see how God used those circumstances to train me and establish my faith. I am much more confident that God will never leave or forsake me and that I can endure any storm because of the strength of the Lord and His desire to provide it. It is important that you show grace to yourself by not expecting perfection even in your storms. You likely would never expect a friend to weather a storm perfectly; why would you expect it of yourself?

Even the apostle Paul had to grow in his trust in the Lord. Notice what he says in 2 Timothy 1:12: "For I know whom I have believed and am persuaded that he is able to keep that which I have committed unto him against that day" (NKJV). Paul had to be persuaded of God's abilities, which means he wasn't convinced at first. But once the persuasion was established, he walked in confidence and rest, knowing God could be trusted.

This kind of rest empowered Paul to endure any circumstance seeking to steal, kill, or destroy his faith. True rest gives you the ability to look any storm in the face and command the waters to be still. True rest empowers its host to stand with a posture so strong that no enemy can withstand it. True rest empowers you to be "more than conquerors through Him who loved us." (Romans 8:37, NIV) True rest fills you with God's grace.

12

A LIFE OF EXCELLENCE

Faith Versus Fear

I t's easy to read this book and conclude that it is unhealthy to have high standards, but that could not be further from the truth! Having a high standard of excellence in all that you do is not necessarily a bad thing.

Take, for instance, your career. Studies show that perfectionists tend to hold certain qualities in the workplace that many employers appreciate: They tend to be motivated, willing to work long hours to get things done right, ready to go the extra mile, and take care in ensuring details are accurate, to name a few.[20] Those with high standards of excellence care about getting the job done and getting it done well.

Excellence is valued in Scripture. Peter exhorts the church, "applying all diligence, in your faith supply *moral excellence*, and in your moral excellence, knowledge." (2 Peter 1:5, NASB) And in another place: "*Keep your behavior excellent* among the Gentiles, so that in the thing in which they slander you as evildoers, they may because of your good deeds, as they observe them, glorify God in the day of visitation." (1 Peter 2:12, NASB)

I remember the year I was working at a local public institution of higher education and had been supervising a multi-million-dollar grant. I was in charge of planning a closeout event that would highlight the outcomes and successes in partnership with local stakeholders. It was a huge undertaking that involved everything from creating the invitation list to choosing the venue, creating program materials, picking the hors d'oeuvres, and creating a video and fireside chat. You would have thought I had obtained a job as an event planner! To say I strove for excellence in every aspect of that event would be an understatement. I operate from the belief that impressions matter. In this case, hundreds of individuals would evaluate our program to determine if they would fund future iterations. It mattered that we left an excellent impression, as it would influence the future for so many. To this day, people still rave about how incredible that event was. It made a lasting impression, and portions of it were funded several years after.

I believe that the biggest difference between perfectionism and standards of excellence is in the motives behind them. According to the Harvard Business Review, excellence crosses a line into perfectionism when you "set inflexible and excessively high standards, you hold an all-or-nothing mindset about your performance ('my work is either perfect or a total failure'), and your self-worth is contingent on performing perfectly."[20]

Have you ever known someone attending college classes who could not accept a grade lower than an A on anything? And if it did happen, that person believed he or she was a complete failure? On the other hand, a person who strives to do the best he or she can, prepares as much as humanly possible, gets a B, and, though somewhat disappointed, still celebrates it, has found a more excellent way.

I love what Sharon Fletcher says in a post from her blog, "Refreshing Moments with Sharon Fletcher."

"When something is done in pursuit of excellence, you have the desire to do your very best with the resources, gifts, and talents that you have. This is fueled by the love you have for God and the love you have for people, and your faith that He will accomplish what needs to be accomplished after you have given your all.

When something is done in pursuit of perfection, you still have the desire to do your very best. But the fuel behind it is not so clean. This is fueled by the fear of what others will think, or what others will say. It is fueled by the desire for acceptance, and the fear of rejection. Or, even worse, we become so afraid of what others may think or say that we become paralyzed and do nothing at all. Whatever the case is, perfectionism is never motivated by love or by faith."[21]

I believe God is pleased when our motive is to do the best we can. He encourages us to grow, to add godly qualities to our lives, and to "run the race as if to win." (Philippians 3:12) But Scripture also tells us that "we have this treasure in earthen vessels, that the excellency of the power may be of God, and not of us" (2 Corinthians 4:7, KJV).

Walking free from perfectionism and in the grace of God means you get to improve, grow in the nature of Jesus, and become the very best version of who He intends for you to be. It means that as you pursue excellence out of love for Him and His principles, He can shape and mold you.

> "IT IS GOD WHO ARMS ME WITH STRENGTH, AND MAKES MY WAY PERFECT."
>
> —PSALM 18:32, KJV

As long as you are staying obedient to Him and doing your best in all you do as if you are doing it for Him, He considers that perfect enough.

13

RECEIVING YOUR INHERITANCE

Crossing Over

As I sit here and reflect on what it's like to walk in God's grace and freedom from perfectionism, I cannot help but think of the inheritance that awaits you as you are guided by His Spirit.

If you have walked long enough with Jesus, you know there are times when you reach a crossroads, and your faith is tested. You come to a place where you do not know if you can do what the Father asks you to do. Maybe He is asking you to put down a certain habit that you have held onto and justified or walk away from a relationship that has been a form of security for years. Maybe He shines His light on the true motives of your heart, and you discover that you were only following Him for selfish

> **"FOR I KNOW THE PLANS THAT I HAVE FOR YOU,"**
> **DECLARES THE LORD,**
> **"PLANS FOR PROSPERITY AND NOT FOR DISASTER, TO GIVE YOU A FUTURE AND A HOPE."**
>
> —JEREMIAH 29:11, KJV

reasons. At that point, you battle with whether you can go the distance, and you find yourself considering turning back just as they did in John 6:63–66 when Jesus tells the disciples:

> '*It is the Spirit who gives life*; the flesh profits nothing. The words that I speak to you are spirit, and they are life. But *there are some of you who do not believe.*' For Jesus knew from the beginning who they were who did not believe, and who would betray Him. And He said, 'Therefore I have said to you that no one can come to Me unless it has been granted to him by My Father. *From that time many of His disciples went back and walked with Him no more.*' (NKJV)

These were his disciples. They were no strangers to Jesus; they were His students. They were literally walking with the One who carried the Spirit of the Living God in Him (talk about being led by God's Spirit!), yet the things that Jesus shared must have been too hard for them to accept; therefore, they would much rather return to the comfort of what was familiar. Jesus continued in one direction while they went in an entirely different direction, resulting in a separation from the Lord. This could mean nothing other than that they forfeited their intended destiny because they were unwilling to believe the Lord and trust in His direction.

The Israelites are a perfect example of this. They had been called out of their homeland, Egypt, to a promised land called Canaan, which represented God's rest—that place of peace

> "AND WITHOUT FAITH IT IS IMPOSSIBLE TO PLEASE GOD, BECAUSE ANYONE WHO COMES TO HIM MUST BELIEVE THAT HE EXISTS AND THAT HE REWARDS THOSE WHO EARNESTLY SEEK HIM."
>
> —HEBREWS 11:16, NIV

and freedom from the anguish and distress familiar to them at home, the place of grace I have been talking about. For forty years, God let them wander in the wilderness so they could see what was inside them. Their forgetfulness, disobedience, and unbelief in God's promises continued to provoke God until, eventually, there was an entire generation who would not be allowed to enter the promised land because of their unbelief. (See Hebrews 3:19)

To not enter the promised land of Canaan meant no access to the abundant fertility the land would have provided. Scripture says the land was "flowing with milk and honey" (Exodus 3:8, NIV). There was an inheritance that God wanted to give them. The land was full of blessings and riches that would meet every need and exceed them; a place of protection where they could discover who God created them to be. On the other side of the Jordan River was their destiny, the very thing they chose to forfeit.

Fast forward another forty years, and another generation found themselves at the very same crossroads, only this time nine and a half tribes entered by crossing over the Jordan River. The other two and a half decided they did not want to enter the promised land because they believed the land on the east side of the Jordan River was more fertile, even though it had not been promised to them. They trusted their own viewpoint rather than God's. Their unbelief cost them a hefty price. They exchanged God's protection and perfect will for vulnerability to attack, and eventually, they became slaves in Assyria. They saw fertile land and took it upon themselves to conclude that their way must be better than God's. In essence, they stepped out of God's grace into their own strength. In doing so, they broke relationships with God and their kin and forfeited all they could have had for a short-lived blessing.

* * *

Today I sit here having come to similar crossroads in my own life. There were many moments when I was faced with the decision to fully surrender to God's will and trust that He would provide me the grace to go further with Him. Or I could stay where it was comfortable because I didn't believe it would be any better if I continued with Jesus. Thankfully, the fear of missing my inheritance and being a rule follower always outweighed the desire to remain comfortable; eventually, I surrendered and obeyed. Don't get me wrong; the struggle was real. In some cases, I truly didn't know if I could go on with Jesus. The temptation to appease my worldly appetites or stay comfortable instead of following God's Spirit was almost unbearable at times.

One time in particular comes to mind. It started with a phone call on March 27, 2013.

I was sitting at my desk at a local community college in the supervisor role. It had been a "baptism by fire" kind of role as it held so many firsts for me: leading staff, managing a federal grant, running a budget, working in higher education, and working for a state institution. There were many things to think about, from regulatory and compliance, marketing and outreach, relationship building in the community, quality assurance and continuous improvement, coordinating graduations, and helping students find jobs. It was multidimensional, fast-paced, enjoyable, and often stressful, but I loved it, and God showed me much through it.

Just about the time I was finally comfortable and feeling like I was starting to know what I was doing, the phone rang.

"Hey, Leneé, it's Lisa!" Lisa had worked for me under the grant but then moved into a full-time position as a career services director for a local career college.

"Hey, Lisa! So great to hear from you! What's going on? How are things?" I asked.

"Well, I've got something for you," she said. "Paula, our campus president, is retiring. What do you think about being a campus president?"

"Huh? Why in the world are you calling me?" I replied. That was literally my response. But even as I prayed, I knew I was to explore this opportunity, and by August 2013, I was resigning from one college to start working as a campus president for another.

Campus president? I was so frightened. You should have seen what I wrestled through during the months leading up to the hiring decision. Fear was the topic of each day as I was tossed to and fro by each wave that hit me; I was driven by my emotions. My stress levels were constantly heightened; I could barely find room in my mind to be present because I was filled with all of the "what ifs" and "why me's," the "but what abouts" and the "but Gods." Campus president? Are you serious, God? I only just began pursuing an MBA, let alone a Ph.D., and I'm so *non*-academic in nature. How could you possibly think that I'm the best fit for this?! "God, please don't make me do this!" I cried.

God chose me. The fact that I was even considered for the role of campus president was divine. You see, I had never been a campus president. I had never worked in proprietary education. I had never led that many people in my entire life. I had only been a one-time supervisor of a small staff. I knew nothing of academic compliance, educational accreditation, state subsidies, or loan defaults. I was just a nobody, trying to tell everybody about somebody who saved my soul. (*Wink, wink.* Any Casting Crowns fans out there?) I was a woman after God's own heart, and I did all I could to be the best I could be for my company, colleagues, students, community, and Him.

Yet none of that mattered. You see, the Lord was going to have His way and let His Light shine, not according to man's wisdom but according to His divine power. Just as He chose David to conquer Goliath, he chose me to be campus president. Not according to the principles of man such as needing to have the proper credentials or having a degree from the right school or even having previous experience in that role; no, those are the outer appearance things that man looks for. But while man looks upon those, God is busy looking upon the heart (See 1 Sam 16:7), and God chooses according to what He sees within our hearts both now and in the future.

It's not that God didn't hear my cries. It's not that God didn't care about my feelings. But He also knows what He is capable of and how the circumstance He is asking us to walk into will serve to usher in His destiny for us and those around us. He knows the training, exposure, and experiences necessary to form in us and draw out of us what He intends to use for us and His kingdom.

God knows what He is doing.

Somewhere in the depths of my soul, I knew that if I did not embrace the opportunity before me, I would be aborting any inheritance that awaited me on the other side. I did not know how or what the details meant; I just knew it was the case. I would have to walk in faith and rely on God's grace to fill in the gaps of my inadequacies.

God saw the conflict within, and He never hesitated to run to me with encouragement, vision, and the grace I needed in my times of weakness. He surrounded me with amazing staff members who knew what they were doing. He gave me a vision and strategy for how we could accomplish the tasks at hand. He granted us favor in the community as we walked in integrity and kindness, serving all we came into contact with. Little by little, my trust in Him grew, and my eyes were opened to Him in all new ways. I learned to let Him drive; He revealed Himself to me in greater ways, and our intimacy grew.

Naturally speaking, I had gained more financial resources than ever before, which afforded me amazing opportunities to travel all around the world in addition to the many ways I could bless those in need. I discovered what skills and talents God had given me and where my weaknesses are. I learned how to embrace my mistakes and the mistakes of those around me. I began learning to rest in God's grace rather than on my own strength. My relationship with Him grew stronger; I could sense His presence and hear His still, small voice even more. That one season in time gave me more than I can put into words, none of which would have happened had I not gone the distance with Him. Every opportunity that has since come into my life has built upon the experiences of that one act of obedience, and the physical and spiritual blessings have only become greater. I can say with assurance that going the distance with Jesus is worth everything.

14

CHRIST WITHIN

A Destiny Kind of Intimacy

Christians must realize that salvation is not a destination in itself; it is only the beginning. God's ultimate goal is to form His nature *in* you so that others can find Him *through* you. Check out the words of Paul:

> Since, then, we know what it is to fear the Lord, we try to persuade others. For Christ's love compels us, because we are convinced that one died for all, and therefore all died. And he died for all, that those who live should no longer live for themselves but for him who died for them and was raised again. Therefore, if anyone is in Christ, the new creation has come. The old has gone, the new is here! All this is from God, who reconciled us to himself through Christ and gave us the ministry of reconciliation: that God was reconciling the world to himself in Christ, not counting people's sins against them. And he has committed to us the message of reconciliation. We are therefore Christ's ambassadors, as though God were making his appeal through us.
>
> —2 Corinthians 5:11, 14–15, 18–20, NIV

It is your destiny that you serve as His ambassador and introduce others to their possible destiny through a relationship with Jesus.

The apostle Paul is a great example of someone who entered God's grace and discovered a destiny-like intimacy. Listen to how he describes his transition:

> If anyone else thinks he has reason for confidence in the flesh, I have more: circumcised on the eighth day, of the people of Israel, of the tribe of Benjamin, a Hebrew of Hebrews; as to the law, a Pharisee; as to zeal, a persecutor of the church; as to righteousness under the law, blameless.
>
> —Philippians 3:4–6, ESV

Was Paul confessing to perfectionism? He certainly followed every rule as perfectly as was humanly possible. With confidence, he could call himself blameless, yet He did not know Jesus.

Until he did, and then he declared, "Indeed, I count everything as loss because of the surpassing worth of knowing Christ Jesus my Lord . . . not having a righteousness of my own that comes from the law, but that which comes through faith in Christ, the righteousness from God that depends on faith." (Philippians 3:8–9)

Paul *experienced* Jesus. He had an encounter with the Spirit of the living God that was so undeniable that his only response could be a complete surrender to and acknowledgment of the truth. He accepted that the righteousness that comes through what God did for the sinner is far greater than any righteousness he could walk in. His experience took him beyond intellectual knowledge into an experiential one that created such an intimacy that he declared there is nothing greater than "knowing Christ Jesus my Lord." *He knew Jesus intimately.*

Paul spent the remainder of his years preaching an *indwelling* Christ. He knew that true reconciliation occurred only when there had been an invasion into his soul of the One he encountered.

I distinctly remember my "Saul-like" moment when I had been hotly pursuing God's laws but had not really encountered the Lord on a personal level. Something changed inside of me. It was as if I had heard about Him but had not met Him, and now it was as if He was standing in my kitchen having a conversation with me. All my experiences from that day have been undeniably filled with an awareness of His presence. All that I teach no longer comes from intellectual knowledge of Scripture but rather from actual experiences that are manifestations of those Scriptures.

In A.W. Tozer's book, *God's Pursuit of Man,* he quotes a man named Carlyle who said:

> Only one stipulation do I make: my teacher must know God, otherwise than by hearsay, and Christ must be all in all to him. If a man have only correct doctrine to offer me I am sure to slip out at the first intermission to seek the company of someone who has seen for Himself how lovely is the face of Him who is the Rose of Sharon and the Lily of the Valley. Such a man can help me, and no one else can.[22]

Tozer argues, "History will reveal that the church has gained or lost power exactly as she has moved toward or away from the inwardness of her faith." [23]

For the Gospel to have any power to convert others, it must be accompanied by true experience and knowledge of the One who is its object. Tozer states:

> To seek our divinity merely in books and writings *is to seek the living among the dead;* we do but in vain many

times seek God in these, where His truth too often is not so much enshrined as entombed. He is best discerned by an intellectual touch of Him. *We must see with our eyes, and hear with our ears, and our hands must handle* of the Word of Life. *Nothing can take the place of the touch of God in the soul, and the sense of Someone there.* Real faith, indeed, brings such realization, for *real faith is never the operation of reason* upon texts. Where true faith is, the knowledge of God will be given as fact of consciousness altogether apart from the conclusions of logic. [24]

Consider the Pharisees and Sadducees. They were people who believed in righteousness according to works and not by faith in the Blood of Jesus. Countless times they missed what Jesus was trying to teach them regarding what true life is. He even went so far as to challenge them by saying, "Search the [S]criptures for in them *ye think ye have eternal life*: and they are they which testify of me. And *ye will not come to me, that ye might have life.*" (John 5:39–40, KJV) Tozer describes this empty religiosity well when he says, "While it is never possible to have the Spirit without at least some measure of truth, *it is*, unfortunately, *possible to have the shell of truth without the Spirit.*" [25]

You likely know what it is like to talk with someone who has not really lived the very thing he or she is talking about. For me, those situations have little to no impact, for they do not carry the clout that comes from real-life experience—there is no *power* behind the words.

I shared with you the necessity of being baptized with the Spirit so Christ can dwell *within* you versus exist all around you. The indwelling of Christ enables you to walk in your destiny.

Consider what Jesus said to His apostles before He left Earth:

"Don't you believe that I am in the Father, and that *the Father is in me*? The words I say to you I do not speak on my own authority. Rather, *it is the Father, living in me, who is doing his work.*

"Believe me when I say that I am in the Father and the Father is in me; or at least believe on the evidence of the works themselves.

"Very truly I tell you, whoever believes in me will do the works I have been doing, and they will do even greater things than these, because I am going to the Father."

—John 14:10–12, NIV

Jesus knew it would be more advantageous for Him to leave so that many could receive His Spirit and "do the works" He did! It is exciting to think that you and I have His Spirit living inside us, enabling us to walk as Jesus did on earth.

Important to Jesus's ability to do those works was His relationship with the Father. I quoted John 12:49 earlier in this book, but it is worth repeating: "For I have not spoken of myself; but the Father which sent me, he gave me a commandment, what I should say, and what I should speak." (KJV) Jesus had to be close enough with the Father to know what to say and when to say it.

On the flip side, there will be those who talk the talk of God, absent the relationship, causing the following response from the Lord:

Not every one that saith unto me, Lord, Lord, shall enter into the kingdom of heaven; but he that doeth the will of my Father which is in heaven. Many will say to me in that day, Lord, Lord, have we not prophesied in thy name? and in thy name have cast out devils? and in thy name done many wonderful works? And then will I profess

113

unto them, I never knew you: depart from me, ye that work iniquity.

—Matthew 7:21–23, KJV

On the surface, this section of Scripture may appear confusing, given that the works displayed by these individuals appear Godly and could be considered supernatural; however, those works were not in response to the will of God or from clean motives, as demonstrated by Jesus in John 12:49.

The Father wants to *know* His children, not just have them doing a bunch of works that are considered good, absent a relationship with Him. Doing "many wonderful works" may seem good to many people, yet Jesus denied them.

Do you remember the trees that were in the Garden of Eden? Scripture singles out two trees in particular among every other kind of tree, one of which was the tree of knowledge of good and evil. In Genesis 2:17, God tells Adam and Eve, ". . . of the tree of the knowledge of good and evil, thou shalt not eat of it: for in the day that thou eatest thereof thou shalt surely die." (KJV) It wasn't just a tree of evil; it had good in it, but even good can still be considered rotten fruit because of what it is rooted in.

> **"I AM THE WAY, THE TRUTH AND THE LIFE; NO ONE COMES TO THE FATHER BUT THROUGH ME."**
>
> —JOHN 14:6, NASB

The Tree of Life represents Jesus and is the Tree from which He desires you to eat freely.

The religious people of Jesus's day believed their good works were enough, yet the problem was an issue of their hearts resulting in death. Their pride would not allow the Lord to enter in, bring them new life, and use them as messengers to help save the lives of those around them. They ultimately became the ones who crucified Him.

* * *

The religious root of perfectionism is easily fed by the notion among Christians that they need to "be like Jesus." It launches them into the striving I spoke of earlier, motivated by performance and leaving them absent of the peace and joy brought by true rest in Jesus.

There is much more to Christianity than is taught in the Church today.

I can't say I spent much time reading the book of Revelation during my early years as a Christian, but the reality is that it contains the end of the story and reveals the ultimate purpose of a relationship with Jesus.

Notice what it says in Revelation 19:7. "Let us be glad and rejoice and give honour to him: for *the marriage of the Lamb is come,* and *his wife hath made herself ready.*" (KJV) Marriage is the epitome of intimacy. The Lord is preparing a bride for Himself who will reign with Him for eternity and who has been purified by Him as Paul describes:

> Husbands, love your wives, even as Christ also loved the church, and gave himself for it; *that he might sanctify and cleanse it* with the washing of water by the word, *that he might present it to himself a glorious church, not having spot, or wrinkle, or any such thing; but that it should be holy and without blemish.*
>
> —Ephesians 5:25–27, KJV

When you put faith in Jesus as your Savior, the Seed of His Spirit is planted in you and grows as you learn to cultivate it in the soil of your soul. With your permission, He replaces your nature with His so that you may be a walking testimony of Him; you are part of that bride He is forming. This is the testimony that brings *life* and introduces others to the *person of Jesus Christ*, as opposed to the doctrine of Christianity.

You were born with a purpose. The Lord thought of you when He laid down His life to wash away the consequence of sin and give you the ability to be reconciled back to the Father. He desires to set you free from your burden of perfectionism so that you may discover a grace that enables you to walk through every storm, overcome every principality, and live out your destiny now and for eternity.

> "THE LORD BLESS YOU AND KEEP YOU; THE LORD MAKE HIS FACE SHINE UPON YOU, AND BE GRACIOUS TO YOU; THE LORD LIFT UP HIS COUNTENANCE UPON YOU, AND GIVE YOU PEACE."
>
> —NUMBERS 6:24–26, NKJV

Remember, friend, you WILL make mistakes . . . "yet grace abounds more." (Romans 5:20, KJV)

May you discover true grace as you journey onward.

ENDNOTES

*Unless otherwise indicated, all emphases in quotations are that of the author.

1. Joachim Stoeber & Julian H. Childs, "The Assessment of Self-Oriented and Socially Prescribed Perfectionism: Subscales Make a Difference." *Journal of Personality Assessment 92,* No. 6 (Oct 2010): 577–585, https://doi:10.1080/00223891.2010.513306.

2. Paul L. Hewitt and Gordon L. Flett, "Perfectionism in the Self and Social Contexts: Conceptualization, Assessment, and Association With Psychopathology," *Journal of Personality and Social Psychology 60, No.3 (1991):* 5–31, https://citeseerx.ist.psu.edu/viewdoc/download?doi=10.1.1.320.1494&rep=rep1&type=pdf.

3. Paul L. Hewitt and Gordon L. Flett, "Perfectionism in the Self and Social Contexts: Conceptualization, Assessment, and Association With Psychopathology," *Journal of Personality and Social Psychology 60, no.3 (1991):* 456-470, https://citeseerx.ist.psu.edu/viewdoc/download?doi=10.1.1.320.1494&rep=rep1&type=pdf.

4. Amy Baker, "Picture Perfect: The Problem (Part 1)," April 7, 2014, https://www.

biblicalcounselingcoalition.org/2014/04/07/
picture-perfect-the-problem-part-1/.

5. "The Relationship Purpose of the Ten
Commandments," GodsTenLaws.com, Rules with
Purpose; https://www.godstenlaws.com/purpose/#.
YukHY-zMK3I.

6. Google; Perfect; *Blue Letter Bible*, accessed August 2,
2022, https://www.blueletterbible.org//search/search.
cfm?Criteria=perfect&t=KJV#s=s_primary_0_1.

7. Acts 4:12 (New International Version)
Matthew 7:21–23 (NIV)
Deuteronomy 10:14 (NIV)
Matthew 10:28 (NIV)
Matthew 25:46 (NIV)

8. Encyclopedia Britannica Online, s.v. "Satan," by
Melissa Petruzzello, accessed January 4, 2022, https://
www.britannica.com/topic/Satan.

9. Curt Landry, "What Is a Religious Spirit?"
Spiritual Warfare (blog), *Curt Landry Ministries*,
April 5, 2018, https://www.curtlandry.com/
what-is-a-religious-spirit/.

10. Google; Gospel; *Blue Letter Bible*, accessed August
2, 2022. *https://www.blueletterbible.org//search/search.
cfm?Criteria=gospel&t=KJV#s=s_primary_0_1.*

11. Dietrich Bonhoeffer, *The Cost of Discipleship* (New
York: Simon & Schuster, 1995), 49.

12. Google; Grace; *Blue Letter Bible*, accessed August 2,
2022. https://www.blueletterbible.org//search/search.
cfm?Criteria=grace&t=KJV#s=s_primary_0_1.

13. Google; Abide; *Blue Letter Bible*, accessed August 2, 2022. https://www.blueletterbible.org//search/search.cfm?Criteria=abide&t=KJV#s=s_primary_0_1.

14. Dave Dunham, "When Perfectionism Is Sin," *Reflections on Biblical Soul Care (blog) Pastor Dave Online* (blog), September 17, 2014, https://pastordaveonline.org/2014/09/17/when-perfectionism-is-sin/.

15. Rick Thomas, "The Torment of Perfectionism," April 17, 2012, https://www.biblicalcounselingcoalition.org/2012/04/17/the-torment-of-perfectionism/.

16. Jill Rosen, "Writing and Speaking Are Totally Separate in the Brain," *Futurity (blog)*, May 13, 2015, https://www.futurity.org/brains-speech-writing-communication-919852/.

17. Google; Renewing; *Blue Letter Bible*, accessed August 2, 2022, https://www.blueletterbible.org//search/search.cfm?Criteria=renewing&t=KJV#s=s_primary_0_1.

18. Rick Phillips, "Why was David's Census a Great Sin?" *Tenth Presbyterian Church* (blog), July 28, 2002, https://www.tenth.org/resource-library/articles/why-was-davids-census-a-great-sin/.

19. Google; Gospel; *Blue Letter Bible*, accessed August 2, 2022. https://www.blueletterbible.org/search/search.cfm?Criteria=rest&t=KJV#s=s_primary_0_1.

20. Brian Swider, Dana Harari, Amy P. Breidenthal, and Laurens Bujold Steed, "The Pros and Cons of Perfectionism, According to Research," *Harvard Business Review* (blog), December 27, 2018, https://hbr.org/2018/12/

the-pros-and-cons-of-perfectionism-according-to-research.

21. Sharon Fletcher, "Freedom from Perfection," *Refreshing Moments* (blog), September 25, 2018, https://www.refreshingmomentswithsharon.com/blog/2018/9/17/freedom-from-perfection.

22. A. W. Tozer, *God's Pursuit of Man* (Chicago: Moody Publishers, 2015), 342.

23. Tozer, A.W. *God's Pursuit of Man*. Chicago, IL. Moody Publishers.

24. Ibid.

25. Ibid.

ABOUT THE AUTHOR

Leneé Pezzano is an author, speaker, and professional mentor whose greatest mission is to evangelize God's truth in such a way as to restore His principles in the earth and inspire individuals to an authentic relationship with Him. Leneé has walked with Jesus for almost thirty years, impacting hundreds of individuals across multiple platforms. She was born and raised in Ohio and resides there still. When Leneé is not working a day job, running a side business, or studying God's Word, she can be found spending time with friends, traveling, hiking, riding her motorcycle, or dancing. Connect with her at LeneePezzano.com.

INVITE LENEÉ PEZZANO TO
SPEAK AT YOUR NEXT EVENT

Leneé Pezzano is a dynamic and authentic speaker who offers a wealth of personal growth resources for your events:

- Conferences
- Retreats
- Coaching
- Group Studies

Connect with Leneé and learn more at LeneePezzano.com.